W9-AOB-729

Helping Students Understand Pre-Algebra

By

BARBARA SANDALL, Ed.D., & MARY SWARTHOUT, Ph.D.

COPYRIGHT © 2005 Mark Twain Media, Inc.

ISBN   10-digit: 1-58037-294-5
          13-digit: 978-1-58037-294-7

Printing No. CD-404021

Mark Twain Media, Inc., Publishers
Distributed by Carson-Dellosa Publishing LLC

Visit us at www.carsondellosa.com

Table of Contents

Table of Contents

Introduction to the Helping Students Understand Algebra Series

The *Helping Students Understand Algebra Series* will introduce students in middle school and/or high school to the course topics of Pre-Algebra, Algebra I, and Algebra II. All of the worktexts are aligned with the National Council of Teachers of Mathematics (NCTM) *Principles and Standards for School Mathematics*.

This series is written for classroom teachers, parents, families, and students. The worktexts in this series can be used as full units of study or as individual lessons to supplement textbooks or curriculum programs. Parents and students can use this series as an enhancement to what is being done in the classroom or as a tutorial at home. All students will benefit from these activities, but the series was designed with the struggling math student in mind. The **concepts and explanations** for the concepts are described in simple **step-by-step instructions** with **examples** in the introduction of each lesson. Students will be given practice problems using the concepts introduced and descriptions of real-life applications of the concepts.

According to the Mathematics Education Trust and the NCTM, new technologies requiring the fundamentals of algebra and algebraic thinking should be a part of the educational background of all citizens. These technologies also provide opportunities to generate numerical examples, graph data, analyze patterns, and make generalizations. An understanding of algebra is also important because business and industry require higher levels of thinking and problem solving.

The NCTM *Standards* suggest content and vocabulary are necessary, but of equal importance are the processes of mathematics. The process skills described in the *Standards* include problem solving, reasoning, communication, and connections. The worktexts in this series will address both the content and processes of algebra and algebraic thinking. This worktext, *Helping Students Understand Pre-Algebra* will help students transition from arithmetic to algebra.

Principles and Standards for School Mathematics, NCTM

Number and Operations
Students will be enabled to:
- Understand numbers, ways of representing numbers, relationships among numbers, and number systems.
- Understand meanings of operations and how they relate to one another.
- Compute fluently and make reasonable estimates.

Algebra
Students will be enabled to:
- Understand patterns, relations, and functions.
- Represent and analyze mathematical situations and structures using algebraic symbols.
- Use mathematical models to represent and understand quantitative relationships.
- Analyze change in various contexts.

Geometry
Students will be enabled to:
- Analyze characteristics and properties of two- and three-dimensional geometric shapes and develop mathematical arguments about geometric relationships.
- Specify locations and describe spatial relationships using coordinate geometry and other representational systems.
- Apply transformations and use symmetry to analyze mathematical situations.
- Use visualization, spatial reasoning, and geometric modeling to solve problems.

Measurement
Students will be enabled to:
- Understand measurable attributes of objects and the units, systems, and processes of measurement.
- Apply appropriate techniques, tools, and formulas to determine measurements.

Data Analysis and Probability
Students will be enabled to:
- Formulate questions that can be addressed with data and collect, organize, and display relevant data to answer them.
- Select and use appropriate statistical methods to analyze data.
- Develop and evaluate inferences and predictions that are based on data.
- Understand and apply basic concepts of probability.

NCTM Standards and Expectations
Grades 6–8 Algebra, NCTM

Algebra Instructional programs grades 6–8 should enable all students to—

Understand patterns, relations, and functions.
- Represent, analyze, and generalize a variety of patterns with tables, graphs, words, and when possible symbolic rules.
- Relate and compare different forms of representation for a relationship.
- Identify functions as linear or nonlinear and contrast their properties from tables, graphs, or equations.

Represent and analyze mathematical situations and structures using algebraic symbols.
- Develop an initial conceptual understanding of different uses of variables.
- Explore relationships between symbolic expressions and graphs of lines, paying particular attention to the meaning of intercept and slope.
- Use symbolic algebra to represent situations and solve problems, especially those that involve linear relationships.
- Recognize and generate equivalent forms for simple algebraic expressions and solve linear equations.

Use mathematical models to represent and understand quantitative relationships.
- Model and solve contextualized problems using various representations, such as graphs, tables, and equations.

Analyze change in various contexts.
- Use graphs to analyze the nature of changes in quantities in linear relationships.

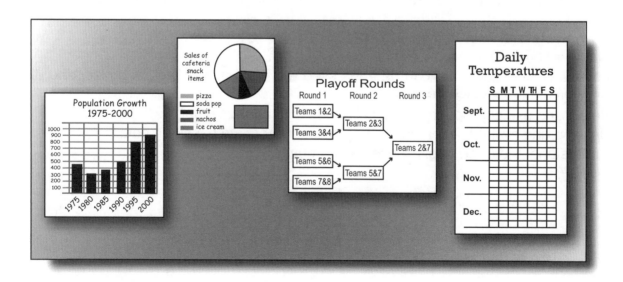

Common Mathematics Symbols and Terms

Term	Symbol/Definition	Example
Addition sign	+	$2 + 2 = 4$
Subtraction sign	−	$4 - 2 = 2$
Multiplication sign	x or a dot • or 2 numbers or letters together or parentheses	3×2 $2 \cdot 2$ $2x$ $2(2)$
Division sign	÷ or a slash mark (/) or a horizontal fraction bar, or $\overline{}$	$6 \div 2$ $4/2$ $\frac{4}{2}$ $2\overline{)4}$
Equals or is equal to	=	$2 + 2 = 4$
Does Not Equal	≠	$5 \neq 1$
Parentheses – symbols for grouping numbers	( )	$(2 \times 5) + 3 =$
Pi – a number that is approximately $\frac{22}{7}$ or ≈ 3.14	π	$3.1415926\ldots$
Negative number – to the left of zero on a number line	−	-3
Positive number – to the right of zero on a number line	+	+4
Less than	<	$2 < 4$
Greater than	>	$4 > 2$
Greater than or equal to	≥	$2 + 3 \geq 4$
Less than or equal to	≤	$2 + 1 \leq 4$
Is approximately equal to	≈	$\pi \approx 3.14$
Radical sign	$\sqrt{}$	$\sqrt{9}$ The square root of 9 $\sqrt[3]{27}$ The cube root of 27
The nth power of a	a^n	$3^2 = 9$

Common Mathematics Symbols and Terms (cont.)

Variable	A letter used for an unknown number	$x + 8 = 12$ x is the letter representing the unknown number or variable
Mathematical Sentence	Contains two mathematical phrases joined by an equals (=) or an inequalities ($\neq, <, >, \leq, \geq$) sign	$2 + 3 = 5$ $9 - 3 > 5$ $3x + 8 = 20$
Equation	Mathematical sentence in which two phrases are connected with an equals (=) sign.	$5 + 7 = 12$ $3x = 12$ $1 = 1$
Mathematical Operations	Mathematics has four basic operations: addition, subtraction, multiplication, and division. Symbols are used for each operation.	+ sign indicates addition – sign indicates subtraction ÷ indicates division • or x indicates multiplication
Like Terms	Can be all numbers or variables that are the same letter and same exponent	$3, 4, 5$ $3c, -5c, \frac{1}{2}c$ the variable is the same with the same exponent; they are like terms
Unlike Terms	Can be numbers or variables that are different	$5 + a$ Cannot be added because they are unlike terms $3x + 4y + 1z$ cannot be added because the variables are different, so they are unlike terms
Coefficient	The number in front of the variable (letter for the unknown number)	$5x$ In this number, 5 is the coefficient.
Identity Property of Addition	Any number or variable added to zero is that number or variable.	$0 + 5 = 5$ $-3 + 0 = -3$ $a + 0 = a$
Identity Property of Multiplication	Any number or variable times 1 is equal to that number or variable.	$12 \cdot 1 = 12$ $b \cdot 1 = b$ $3y \cdot 1 = 3y$

Common Mathematics Symbols and Terms (cont.)

Commutative Property of Addition	No matter the order in which you add two numbers, the sum is always the same.	$4 + 7 = 7 + 4$ $b + c = c + b$
Commutative Property of Multiplication	No matter what order you multiply two numbers, the answer is always the same.	$20 \times \frac{1}{2} = \frac{1}{2} \times 20$ $5 \cdot 3 = 3 \cdot 5$ $a \cdot b = b \cdot a$
Associative Property of Addition	When you add three numbers together, the sum will be the same no matter how you group the numbers.	$(5 + 6) + 7 = 5 + (6 + 7)$ $(a + b) + c = a + (b + c)$
Associative Property of Multiplication	No matter how you group the numbers when you multiply, the answer will always be the same product.	$(5 \cdot 4) \cdot 8 = 5 \cdot (4 \cdot 8)$ $(a \cdot b) \cdot c = a \cdot (b \cdot c)$
Distributive Property of Multiplication Over Addition	Allows the choice of multiplication followed by addition or addition followed by multiplication.	$3(5 + 2) = 3 \cdot 5 + 3 \cdot 2$ $a(b + c) = a \cdot b + a \cdot c$
Inverse Operation	Operation that cancels another operation	Multiplication and division $5 \cdot x = 5x$ $\dfrac{5x}{5} = x$ Addition and Subtraction $n + 5 - 5 = n$
Reciprocal or Multiplicative Inverse Property	Two numbers are multiplied, and the product is 1.	For any non-zero number: Number $\times \dfrac{1}{\text{Number}} = 1$ $\dfrac{1}{\text{Number}} \times$ Number $= 1$ $a \cdot \dfrac{1}{a} = 1$ $5 \cdot \dfrac{1}{5} = 1$

Common Mathematics Symbols and Terms (cont.)

Exponents	Shorthand for repeated multiplication	$a^2 = a \bullet a$ $y^4 = y \bullet y \bullet y \bullet y$
Square Numbers	The result of multiplying a number or variable by itself	$4 \bullet 4 = 16$ $a \bullet a = a^2$
Square Roots	A square root indicated by the radical sign $\sqrt{}$ is the number multiplied by itself to get the radicand.	$\sqrt{9}$ What number multiplied by itself = 9? $3 \bullet 3 = 9$ So $\sqrt{9} = 3$
Radicand	Number under the radical	$\sqrt{9}$ 9 is the radicand
Numerator	Top number in a fraction	$\frac{3}{5}$ In this fraction, 3 is the numerator
Denominator	Bottom number in a fraction	$\frac{3}{5}$ In this fraction, 5 is the denominator
Integers	Natural numbers, their opposites, or negative numbers, and zero	Set of Integers: $\{...-3,-2,-1,0,1,2,3...\}$
Additive Inverse Property of Addition	The sum of an integer and its opposite integer will always be zero.	$a + -a = 0$ $5 + -5 = 0$
Set	Specific group of numbers or objects	Set of Integers: $\{...-3,-2,-1,0,1,2,3...\}$
Absolute Value	$\lvert a \rvert$ The absolute value of a number can be considered as the distance between the number and zero on a number line. The absolute value of every number will be either positive or zero. Real numbers come in paired opposites, a and $-a$, that are the same distance from the origin, but in opposite directions.	Absolute value of a If a is a positive, $\lvert a \rvert = a$. If a is a negative, $\lvert a \rvert = a$. If a is 0, $\lvert a \rvert = 0$. If 0 is the origin on the number line on the left, 3 is the absolute value of the pair -3 and +3, because they are both 3 marks from 0.

-3 -2   -1   0   1   2 3

Chapter 1: Basic Concepts of Numbers

Introduction to the Concepts of Numbers

This section is a review of the basic mathematical concepts needed prior to learning algebra. According to the NCTM *Standards*, students need to be able to:

- Understand numbers, ways of representing numbers, relationships among numbers, and number systems. NCTM.

Galileo said, "[The universe] cannot be read until we have learned the language and become familiar with the characters in which it is written." In order to understand algebra, you need to understand the language of algebra. Algebra uses numbers, symbols, and letters. The numbers used in algebra include the types of numbers described in this section. Different symbols, shown in the chart on the previous pages, mean different things. All of the symbols used in mathematics help describe the numbers or the operations to be done. The letters (variables) used in mathematics represent unknown numbers. This chapter examines types of numbers used in algebra. More detail will be provided as you work your way through this worktext.

Concepts

1 Types of Numbers

    A Natural Numbers

    B Whole Numbers

    C Integers

    D Rational Numbers (Fractions)

    E Irrational Numbers

    F Real Numbers

Chapter 1: Basic Concepts of Numbers (cont.)

Explanations of Concepts

1 **Types of Numbers**

The major types of numbers described in this worktext include natural numbers, whole numbers, integers, rational numbers, irrational numbers, and real numbers.

A **Natural Numbers**

Natural numbers are sometimes called **counting numbers** because they are the numbers you use to count how many items you have. Zero is not included in the set of natural numbers. TIP: One way to remember this is if you did not have any items, you could not count them.

Example:

Counting the oranges below you would count 1, 2, 3, so you have 3 oranges.

1   2   3

= 3 oranges

Examples of other natural numbers:

8   162   1,723   5

Examples of numbers that are not natural numbers:

0   0.35   -2 $\frac{4}{7}$

Chapter 1: Basic Concepts of Numbers (cont.)

B   Whole Numbers

Whole numbers include the natural numbers and zero.

Examples of whole numbers:

0	28	1,005

Examples of numbers that are not whole numbers:

-2	0.45	$\frac{4}{5}$

Look at the number line below. The numbers represented by the equally spaced marks to the right of zero are whole numbers. The arrow on the number line indicates that the line goes on forever or to infinity. Any number that is between the marks would not be a whole number.

C   Integers

Integers are natural numbers, their opposites or negative numbers, and zero. All whole numbers are integers and all natural numbers can be called integers.

Examples of integers:

-4	0	-57	2,356	+4

Examples of numbers that are not integers:

$\frac{1}{2}$	$3\frac{1}{4}$	0.75	-11.46

Look at the number line below. The negative numbers have been added to the previous number line. The numbers represented by the equally spaced marks to the left or right of zero are integers. Any number represented between the marks is not an integer. For example, 1.5 is not an integer.

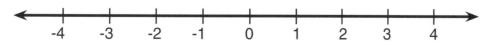

Chapter 1: Basic Concepts of Numbers (cont.)

D   **Rational Numbers (Fractions)**

A rational number is a number that can be expressed as the ratio of two integers. This ratio is sometimes called a **fraction**. The set of rational numbers includes the integers, whole numbers, and natural numbers that were discussed earlier. Decimals are rational numbers if the decimal has a finite number of places in it or it repeats a block of digits infinitely. To find the decimal form of $\frac{1}{2}$, divide the numerator (in this case it is 1) by the denominator (in this case it is 2). The decimal form of $\frac{1}{2} = 0.5$.

Examples of rational numbers:

3 is a rational number because it can be written as $\frac{3}{1}$.

$\frac{1}{4}$ $\frac{2}{3}$ 0.35   5.2345   0.5

0.272727… or it can be written as $0.\overline{27}$, is a repeating decimal. It is a rational number because it repeats the same finite block of numbers forever or to infinity.

Example of a decimal that is <u>not</u> a rational number:

π is the symbol for pi. The decimal form of pi is 3.1415926…

0.01011011101111… and it continues. This pattern never ends, but it does not repeat the same finite block of digits, so it is not a rational number.

E   **Irrational Numbers**

Irrational numbers are numbers that cannot be expressed as a ratio of two integers. The square root of two is an example of an irrational number. An irrational number can be defined as a decimal that never repeats and never ends. The square root of any number that is not a perfect square will be irrational. The square root of 16 ($\sqrt{16}$) is 4, and 4 is a rational number. $\sqrt{3} = 1.7320508….$ This is a decimal that never repeats the same finite block of digits and never ends, so it is an irrational number.

Chapter 1: Basic Concepts of Numbers (cont.)

Examples of irrational numbers:

$$\sqrt{2} \qquad\qquad \sqrt{3}$$

π is the symbol for pi. The decimal form of pi is 3.1415926… .

0.01011011101111… and it continues. This pattern never ends, and it never repeats the same finite block of digits.

Examples of numbers that are not irrational numbers:

$$\sqrt{16}$$

-15

$$-\frac{7}{32}$$

F   **Real Numbers**

Real numbers are a combination of all the number systems. Real numbers include natural numbers, whole numbers, integers, rational numbers, and irrational numbers. Examples of real numbers could be any number. Examples of each were shown above.

Chapter 1: Basic Concepts of Numbers (cont.)

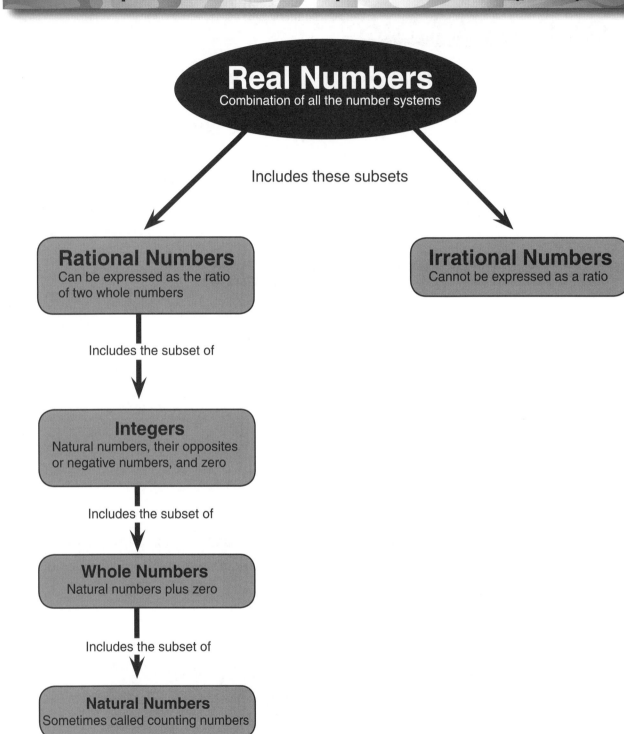

Real Numbers
Combination of all the number systems

Includes these subsets

Rational Numbers
Can be expressed as the ratio
of two whole numbers

Irrational Numbers
Cannot be expressed as a ratio

Includes the subset of

Integers
Natural numbers, their opposites
or negative numbers, and zero

Includes the subset of

Whole Numbers
Natural numbers plus zero

Includes the subset of

Natural Numbers
Sometimes called counting numbers

Name: _____ Date: _____

Chapter 1: Basic Concepts of Numbers (cont.)

Practice: Which Number Is Which?

Directions: Using the words listed below, fill in blanks with the correct number type(s).

Real Number	Rational Number	Integer	Whole Number
Natural Number	Irrational Number		

Number   **Type or Types**

1. 8   _____

2. 0   _____

3. -6   _____

4. $\frac{1}{4}$ _____

5. -450   _____

6. $\sqrt{9}$ _____

7. $-\frac{21}{23}$ _____

8. 0.12122122212222…   _____

9. $0.\overline{0367}$ _____

10. $\sqrt{11}$ _____

Name: _____   Date: _____

Chapter 1: Basic Concepts of Numbers (cont.)

Practice: Numbers—Are They Real?

Directions: Use the clues below to complete the crossword puzzle about the types of numbers discussed in this chapter.

ACROSS

4. Natural numbers, their opposites or the negative numbers, and zero
7. Can be expressed as a ratio of two whole numbers
9. A ratio of two integers
10. A _____ that never repeats the same finite block of digits and never ends is an irrational number.

DOWN

1. This number is not included in the natural numbers, but it is a whole number.
2. Another name for natural numbers
3. The natural numbers plus zero
5. These numbers are sometimes called counting numbers.
6. A combination of all of the number systems
8. These numbers cannot be expressed as a ratio.

Directions: Give an example of each of the six number systems.

1. _____   2. _____   3. _____

4. _____   5. _____   6. _____

Chapter 1: Basic Concepts of Numbers (cont.)

Summary of Numbers

All types of numbers are needed in working to solve problems. Algebra uses numbers, symbols, and letters to solve problems. Types of numbers described in this section include real, rational, irrational, integers, whole, and natural.

- Real Numbers are a combination of all the number systems.
- Rational Numbers can be expressed as the ratio of two whole numbers.
- Irrational Numbers cannot be expressed as a ratio.
- Integers include natural numbers, their opposites or negative numbers, and zero.
- Whole Numbers are the natural numbers plus zero.
- Natural Numbers are sometimes called counting numbers.

Tip to Remember

An easy way to understand how these number systems fit together is to look at a number line. Real numbers, or all of the number systems discussed in this section, make up all of the numbers represented by the marks with numbers and all of the points in between the marks. Remember that the arrows indicate that this number line goes on into infinity or forever in both directions.

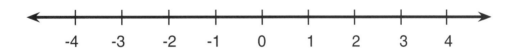

Real Life Applications of Numbers

Numbers are used in a variety of ways in everyday life. Counting materials and foods, determining the number of miles per gallon of gasoline, measuring material such as wood and cloth, finding the masses and weights of fruits and vegetables in the grocery store, and measuring volume of ingredients when cooking are all applications of numbers.

Chapter 2: Operations of Numbers and Variables

Introduction to Operations of Numbers and Variables

This section is a continuation of the review of the basic mathematical concepts needed prior to learning algebra. According to the NCTM *Standards*, students need to be able to:

- Understand meanings of operations and how they relate to one another.
- Compute fluently and make reasonable estimates.

    NCTM.

Algebra uses numbers, symbols and letters. This section describes the operations of numbers and variables. Different symbols, shown in the table in the beginning of this worktext, mean different things. All symbols help describe the operations to be completed in doing the problem. A letter represents an unknown number or quantity. This is called a **variable**. All of these will be described in more detail as you work your way through this worktext.

Concepts

1 Operations of Numbers and Variables

    A Addition

    B Subtraction

    C Multiplication

    D Division

    E Zero

    F Order of Operations

$$7(8+2) \div 65 - 5 =$$

$$(3 \div 2) + (6 \cdot 8) =$$

$$9x + 4 - 16 \div 2 + 10 =$$

Chapter 2: Operations of Numbers and Variables (cont.)

Explanations of Concepts of Numbers and Variables

1 **Operations of Numbers and Variables**

Mathematics has four basic number and variable operations: addition, subtraction, multiplication, and division. The operations listed are used to act on terms. A **term** can be a number (like 6), it can be a variable (like m), or it can be a product or quotient of numbers and variables (like 6m or $\frac{7m}{8y}$). At times, we need to know if terms can be called **like terms**. For example, $12xy$ and $-7xy$ are like terms because their variable parts are exactly alike. An example of terms that are unlike would be 12xy and $-7x^2y$. The variables used are the same (x's and y's), but in one term, the x is raised to the second power—that causes the terms to be unlike. In a term that combines numbers and variables, the number part is called the **coefficient**. For example, in the term $12xy$, the coefficient would be 12. As the review of operations will remind you, knowing like terms from unlike terms and the meaning of the coefficient is important to being able to work with numbers, variables, and operations.

Symbols are used to indicate what operation is to be used in solving the problem.
+ Sign indicates addition
− Sign indicates subtraction
$\div$, /, or $\sqrt{}$ Indicates division
x, ( ), or • Indicates multiplication

A **Addition**
When doing addition, only add like terms. Like terms mean any number or variable that uses the same letter. When you add variables that are the same, you add the coefficients or the numbers in front of the variables.

Examples of adding like terms:

$21 + 34 = 55$ $3x + 6x = 9x$

3 apples   +   7 apples   =   10 apples

Chapter 2: Operations of Numbers and Variables (cont.)

Examples of adding coefficients: (**Note:** The variables, the letters representing the unknown numbers, are the same in each equation.):

$$3x + 6x = 9x \qquad\qquad \tfrac{1}{3}a + 4a + 7a = 11\tfrac{1}{3}a$$

$$y + 2y = 3y \quad \text{(The coefficient of the first } y \text{ is 1.)}$$

4 fruit	+	5 fruit	+	6 fruit	=	15 fruit

Unlike terms cannot be added. They include a number and letter, or two or more different variables.

Examples of phrases with unlike terms that cannot be added:

$$5 + x = \qquad\qquad 5x + 3y + 2z =$$

3 apples	+	4 oranges	+	8 bananas	=

B Subtraction

Only like terms can be subtracted. One number can be subtracted from another and one variable (unknown number represented by a letter) can be subtracted from another, if they are the same variable.

Example of subtraction of like terms:

You have five candy bars. If you eat two of them, how many do you have?

5 candy bars	–	2 candy bars eaten	=	3 candy bars left	$5 - 2 = 3$

Remember, unlike terms cannot be subtracted.

Example of phrase with unlike terms:

$5x - 5y$ (Cannot be solved because there are two different variables.)

18

Name: _____ Date: _____

Chapter 2: Operations of Numbers and Variables (cont.)

Practice: Addition and Subtraction of Numbers and Variables

Directions: Perform the following operations. If you cannot perform the operation, explain why the operation cannot be done.

1. $335 + 1{,}567 =$ _____

2. $3a + 12a + 1a =$ _____

3. $3a + 24b + 4c =$ _____

4. $8x + 9x =$ _____

5. $\frac{1}{2}x + 5x =$ _____

6. $5a + a =$ _____

7. $18 + 9 =$ _____

8. $8 + c =$ _____

9. $4x - 8y =$ _____

10. $35 - 10 =$ _____

11. $7 - \frac{1}{2} =$ _____

12. $123a - 5a =$ _____

13. $2{,}345 - 5z =$ _____

14. $435a - 37a =$ _____

Chapter 2: Operations of Numbers and Variables (cont.)

C   **Multiplication of Numbers and Variables**

Any like or unlike terms can be multiplied. Numbers or variables can be multiplied. A number times a variable or coefficients can be multiplied.

Examples of multiplying two numbers or variables:

If you have two students, and each has five cookies and they put them together, how many do you have?

2 students   x   5 cookies   =   10 cookies   2 x 5 = 10

Examples of multiplying two variables (two unknown numbers):

$a \bullet b = ab$ $y \bullet y = y^2$ (y squared)

Examples of multiplying numbers times variables:

$5 \bullet a = 5a$ $8 \bullet b = 8b$

> Remember, the **dot** can also be used as a **multiplication** sign.

Examples of multiplying unlike terms:

Multiply the coefficients together, and then put the variable at the end of the answer.

Problem:	$3 \bullet 6y =$
Step 1: Multiply the coefficients.	$3 \bullet 6 = 18$
Step 2: Put the variable at the end of the answer.	y
Answer:	$3 \bullet 6y = 18y$

Problem:	$2b \bullet 3 =$
Step 1: Multiply the coefficients.	$2 \bullet 3 = 6$
Step 2: Put the variable at the end of the answer.	b
Answer:	$2b \bullet 3 = 6b$

Chapter 2: Operations of Numbers and Variables (cont.)

Multiply two different variables with coefficients. Multiply the coefficients first, and then multiply the variables and combine the two answers.

Problem: $5a \cdot 4c =$

Step 1: Multiply the coefficients. $5 \cdot 4 = 20$

Step 2: Multiply the variables. $a \cdot c = ac$

Step 3: Put the variables at the end of the answer.

Answer: $5a \cdot 4c = 20ac$

Problem: $3z \cdot 5z =$

Step 1: Multiply the coefficients. $3 \cdot 5 = 15$

Step 2: Multiply the variables. $z \cdot z = z^2$

Step 3: Put the variables at the end of the answer.

Answer: $3z \cdot 5z = 15z^2$

Chapter 2: Operations of Numbers and Variables (cont.)

Practice: Multiplication of Numbers and Variables

Directions: Perform the following operations. If the operation cannot be performed, explain why it cannot be done.

1. $7y \cdot 8z =$ _____

2. $27 \cdot 56 =$ _____

3. $10a \cdot 35a =$ _____

4. $a \cdot b =$ _____

5. $22 \cdot 4a =$ _____

6. $b \cdot b =$ _____

7. $5y \cdot 9 =$ _____

8. $25 \cdot 33y =$ _____

9. $21 \cdot b =$ _____

10. $38 \cdot 9 =$ _____

Chapter 2: Operations of Numbers and Variables (cont.)

D **Division**

Like and unlike terms can be divided and so can any two numbers or variables, including different variables. Phrases with numbers and variables can also be divided.

Examples of dividing any two numbers or variables:

$8 \div 4 = 2$ $\qquad\qquad\qquad\qquad\qquad$ $x \div x = 1$

Example of dividing different variables:

$a \div b = \dfrac{a}{b}$

Examples of dividing expressions with numbers (coefficients) and letters:

Divide the coefficients, and then divide the variables. Multiply both answers together.

$\qquad\qquad\qquad\qquad\qquad\qquad\qquad$ **Problem:** $\quad 6a \div 2a =$

Step 1: Divide the coefficients. $\qquad\qquad\qquad$ $6 \div 2 = 3$

Step 2: Divide the variables. $\qquad\qquad\qquad\quad$ $a \div a = 1$

Step 3: Multiply the answers of Steps 1 and 2. $\quad 3 \bullet 1 = 3$

$\qquad\qquad\qquad\qquad\qquad\qquad\qquad$ **Answer:** $\quad 6a \div 2a = 3$

Example of dividing two different variables:

$\qquad\qquad\qquad\qquad\qquad\qquad\qquad$ **Problem:** $\quad 12c \div 3d =$

Step 1: Divide the coefficients. $\qquad\qquad\qquad$ $12 \div 3 = 4$

Step 2: Divide the variables. $\qquad\qquad\qquad\quad$ $c \div d = \dfrac{c}{d}$

Step 3: Multiply the answers of Steps 1 and 2. $\quad 4 \bullet \dfrac{c}{d} = \dfrac{4}{1} \bullet \dfrac{c}{d} = 4\dfrac{c}{d}$

$\qquad\qquad\qquad\qquad\qquad\qquad\qquad$ **Answer:** $\quad 12c \div 3d = 4\dfrac{c}{d}$

Chapter 2: Operations of Numbers and Variables (cont.)

Problem: $9ab \div 3a =$

Step 1: Divide the coefficients. $9 \div 3 = 3$

Step 2: Divide the variables. $ab \div a = \dfrac{ab}{a}$

since $\dfrac{a}{a} = 1$, then $1 \cdot b = b$

Step 3: Multiply the answers of Steps 1 and 2. $3 \cdot b = 3b$

Answer: $9ab \div 3a = 3b$

1800 miles ÷ 50 gallons of gas used = 36 miles per gallon

308 miles ÷ 14 gallons of gas used = 22 miles per gallon

Name: _____ Date: _____

Chapter 2: Operations of Numbers and Variables (cont.)

Practice: Division of Numbers and Variables

Directions: Perform the following operations. If you cannot perform the operation, explain why it cannot be done.

1. $\frac{3}{8} \div \frac{1}{8}$ = _____

2. $800 \div 50$ = _____

3. $36.9 \div 2.4$ = _____

4. $2.5\overline{)37.5}$ = _____

5. $\frac{300}{25}$ = _____

6. $225x \div 3x$ = _____

7. $35x \div 7xy$ = _____

8. $\frac{3x}{4x}$ = _____

9. $\frac{8x}{2y}$ = _____

10. $\frac{8ab}{b}$ = _____

Chapter 2: Operations of Numbers and Variables (cont.)

 Zero

Adding or Subtracting Zero

When adding or subtracting zero and any number or variable, the answer is the number or variable. If you multiply a variable or number by zero, the answer is always zero. Zero divided by any number is zero, but numbers or variables cannot be divided by zero.

Examples of adding or subtracting zero to numbers or variables:

If you have three apples and you add zero apples, how many do you have?

$4 + 0 = 4$ $a + 0 = a$ $2b + 0 = 2b$

If you have three apples and you eat none of them, how many do you have left?

$4 - 0 = 4$ $a - 0 = a$ $2b - 0 = 2b$

Multiplication and Division of Numbers and Variables and Zero

When multiplying a variable or number by zero, the product is always zero. Zero divided by any number is zero; however, a number or variable cannot be divided by zero.

Examples of multiplication by zero:

$5 \bullet 0 = 0$ $a \bullet 0 = 0$ $2a \bullet 0 = 0$

Examples of the division of zero by a number or variable:

$0 \div 5 = 0$ $0 \div a = 0$ $0 \div 4a = 0$ $0 \div (-6) = 0$

You **cannot** divide a number or variable by zero.

$4 \div 0 =$ cannot be divided $a \div 0 =$ cannot be divided

Name: _____ Date: _____

Chapter 2: Operations of Numbers and Variables (cont.)

Practice: Addition, Subtraction, Multiplication, and Division by Zero

Directions: Perform the following operations. If the operation cannot be done, explain why it cannot be done.

1. $5 + 0 =$ _____

2. $0 + \frac{1}{4} =$ _____

3. $0 + y =$ _____

4. $7 - 0 =$ _____

5. $0 - 13 =$ _____

6. $0 - (-12) =$ _____

7. $0 - b =$ _____

8. $55 - 0 =$ _____

9. $a \cdot 0 =$ _____

10. $2{,}000 \cdot 0 =$ _____

11. $8xyz \cdot 0 =$ _____

12. $0 \cdot 9 =$ _____

13. $0 \cdot y =$ _____

14. $0 \cdot \frac{1}{4} =$ _____

15. $0 \div 4 =$ _____

16. $0 \div f =$ _____

17. $3 \div 0 =$ _____

18. $ab \div 0 =$ _____

Chapter 2: Operations of Numbers and Variables (cont.)

F   **Order of Operations for Numbers and Variables**

When solving mathematical expressions that have more than one operation, it is important to do the operations in the correct order.

1. Do the operations in the parentheses. If there are no parentheses, do the operations from left to right.
2. Find the value of any number with an exponent.
3. Multiple or divide first.
4. Add or subtract last.

```
1.  ( )
2.  xⁿ
3.  •  or  ÷
4.  +  or  −
```

Examples of order of operations:

1. Do the operations in the parentheses. If there are no parentheses, do the operations from left to right.

Problem: $8(25 - 5) =$

Step 1: Do the operation in parentheses first. $(25 - 5) = 20$

So the problem is $8(20) =$

Step 2: Then multiply.   **Answer:** $8(20) = 160$

Problem: $5 + (3 \times 5) =$

Step 1: Do the operation in parentheses first. $(3 \times 5) = 15$

Step 2: Then do the addition. $5 + 15 = 20$

Answer: $5 + (3 \times 5) = 20$

2. Find the value of any number with an exponent.

Problem: $5 \times 4^2 =$

Step 1: Find the value of the number with the exponent. $4^2 = 16$

Step 2: Then multiply. $5 \times 16 = 80$

Answer: $5 \times 4^2 = 80$

Chapter 2: Operations of Numbers and Variables (cont.)

Problem: $16 \div 2^2 =$

Step 1: Find the value of the number with the exponent. $2^2 = 4$

Step 2: Then divide. $16 \div 4 = 4$

Answer: $16 \div 2^2 = 4$

3. Multiple or divide first.

4. Then add or subtract

Problem: $8 \times 5 + 4 \times 5 =$

If there are no parentheses, go from left to right.

Step 1: Do the multiplication first. $8 \times 5 = 40; 4 \times 5 = 20$

Step 2: Then do the addition. $40 + 20 = 60$

Answer: $8 \times 5 + 4 \times 5 = 60$

Problem: $25 \div 5 - 24 \div 6 =$

If there are no parentheses, go from left to right.

Step 1: Divide first. $25 \div 5 = 5; 24 \div 6 = 4$

Step 2: Subtract. $5 - 4 = 1$

Answer: $25 \div 5 - 24 \div 6 = 1$

Problem: $6 \times 5 - 4 \times 5 =$

If there are no parentheses, go from left to right.

Step 1: Do the multiplication first. $6 \times 5 = 30; 4 \times 5 = 20$

Step 2: Then do the subtraction. $30 - 20 = 10$

Answer: $6 \times 5 - 4 \times 5 = 10$

Problem: $22 \div 11 + 40 \div 10 =$

If there are no parentheses, go from left to right.

Step 1: Do the division first. $22 \div 11 = 2; 40 \div 10 = 4$

Step 2: Then do the addition. $2 + 4 = 6$

Answer: $22 \div 11 + 40 \div 10 = 6$

Name: _____ Date: _____

Chapter 2: Operations of Numbers and Variables (cont.)

Practice: Order of Operations

Directions: Perform the indicated number operations in the problems that follow. If the operation cannot be done, explain why it cannot be done.

1. $(20 - 2) \div 3 =$ _____

2. $26 + (4 \div 2) =$ _____

3. $3(3 + 5) =$ _____

4. $2(6 - 3) - 3 =$ _____

5. $2 \times 9^2 =$ _____

6. $6 - 3^2 \div 2 =$ _____

7. $3 \times 5 + 4 \times 10 =$ _____

8. $30 \div 5 - 24 \div 6 =$ _____

9. $25 \div 5 + 24 \div 6 =$ _____

10. $3 \times 6 + 4 \times 35 =$ _____

11. $6 \times 5 - 4 \times 5 =$ _____

12. $9 \div 3 - 10 \div 5 =$ _____

13. $3(6 - 3) + 6 \times 2 =$ _____

14. $(6 - 1)^2 - 5 \times 2 =$ _____

15. $6 \div (1 + 2) - 2 =$ _____

16. $10 + 3^2 - 2 + 3 =$ _____

17. $22 - 2 \times 5 + 4 =$ _____

18. $2 - 7(7) + 50 =$ _____

19. $5(6 - 2) - 3 =$ _____

20. $(5 + 6) \times 8 =$ _____

Chapter 2: Operations of Numbers and Variables (cont.)

Practice: Smooth Operator

Directions: Match the symbols with the operation.

_____ **1.** +

_____ **2.** −

_____ **3.** ÷, /, or $\sqrt{}$

_____ **4.** x, ( ), or •

A. Indicates multiplication

B. Indicates subtraction

C. Indicates addition

D. Indicates division

Directions: Match the problem with the operation. Some may match more than one operation.

_____ **5.** Addition

_____ **6.** Subtraction

_____ **7.** Multiplication

_____ **8.** Division

_____ **9.** Addition of Zero

_____ **10.** Multiplication of Zero

_____ **11.** Multiplication by One

A. $675 \times 0 = 0$

B. $66 + 0 = 66$

C. $9{,}876 - 25 = 9{,}851$

D. $99/11 = 9$

E. $3{,}743 \times 1 = 3{,}743$

F. $900(3) = 2{,}700$

G. $789 + 44 = 833$

Directions: Explain the order of operation in each problem.

12. $5(7 + 8) + 8 \times 2$

_____

_____

_____

13. $(9 - 2)^2 - 5 \times 1$

_____

_____

_____

14. $8 \div (4 \times 1) - 1$

_____

_____

_____

15. $(5 - 2)^3 \, (2) + 3$

_____

_____

_____

Chapter 2: Operations of Numbers and Variables (cont.)

Summary of Operations

Algebra uses numbers, symbols, and letters. This section describes the operations of numbers and variables. Different symbols, shown in the table in the beginning of this worktext, mean different things. All symbols help describe the operations to be completed in doing the problem. The letters represent or stand for some number that is unknown. This is called a variable. The number and variable operations in this chapter were addition, subtraction, multiplication, and division. When doing operations with numbers and variables that have more than one operation, it is important to do the operations in the correct order.

Tips to Remember

1. Do the operations in parentheses first.
2. Find the value of any number with an exponent.
3. Multiply and/or divide after the parentheses and exponents are done. If there are no parentheses, do the operations from left to right.
4. Add or subtract last. If there are no parentheses, do the operations from left to right.

Real Life Applications of Operations of Numbers

Number operations and order of operations are applied in bookkeeping, computers, and batting averages.

Chapter 3: Working With Integers and Signed Numbers

Introduction to the Concepts of Integers and Signed Numbers

Why is there a need to expand the number system beyond the whole numbers? What role do the integers and other signed numbers play in dealing with real-world applications of mathematics? Consider a simple situation involving a checking account. Deposits affect the balance of the account in a positive way, and we can think of checks as affecting the balance of the account in a negative way. The hope is that we have more positive than negative action so that the account does not become overdrawn. Dealing with positive and negative numbers, whether integers or not, means the need to think about how to work with whole numbers and how to handle negative values as we add, subtract, multiply, and divide. What is the same? What do we do differently?

Concepts of Integers and Signed Numbers

1 Integers

     Positive Integers

     Negative Integers

2 Absolute Value

3 Additive Inverse Property of Addition

4 Addition of Integers

5 Subtraction of Integers

6 Multiplication of Integers

7 Division of Integers

8 Operating on Signed Numbers

Chapter 3: Working With Integers and Signed Numbers (cont.)

Explanations of Concepts of Integers and Signed Numbers

1 **Integers**

What is an integer? The number line for the whole numbers starts at zero and uses equally spaced marks to represent 1, 2, 3 and the other numbers that belong to the infinite set of whole numbers.

Whole Number Line

With whole numbers, we can handle a lot of situations, but using only whole numbers does not allow us to find an answer to a subtraction problem like 2 – 5 = ___. The set of whole numbers needs to be expanded to form a new set of numbers, called the integers. To do this, we extend the number line below to the left from zero, and place equally spaced marks that are symmetric to the whole number marks, that is, that are the same distance from zero on the left. So, 1 is balanced by -1, 3 is balanced by -3, and so forth so that each whole number has a partner to balance it. Mathematically, we say that each whole number *n* has an opposite or inverse on the number line, **-n**. We can define **the set of integers** as {...,-3, -2, -1, 0, 1, 2, 3, ...} and can illustrate it using a number line.

Integer Number Line

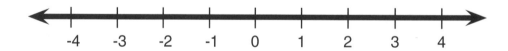

The **positive integers** will be those to the right of zero on the number line. The set of positive integers is {1, 2, 3, ...}. The **negative integers** are those to the left of zero on the number line. The set of negative integers is {-1, -2, -3, ...}. Notice that the number zero is not positive or negative. We can think of zero as neutral—as the buffer that separates the negative and positive integers. The discussion of positive and negative integers leads to the discussion of the absolute value of numbers.

Chapter 3: Working With Integers and Signed Numbers (cont.)

② Absolute Value

The absolute value of a number, *n,* is the answer to the question how far from zero is *n* on the number line? For example, the absolute value of 7, shown symbolically as |7|, would be 7. The absolute value of |-7| is also 7. Examine the number line below. The distance from 0 to 7 is 7 marks and from 0 to -7 is also 7 marks.

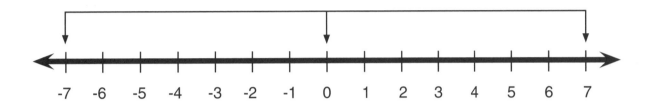

In general, if the number is positive, then the absolute value is the number itself. If it is a negative number, the absolute value is the additive inverse or opposite of that number. The Additive Inverse Property will be discussed in the next section. The absolute value of a quantity is always positive or 0 because it represents a distance.

③ Additive Inverse Property of Addition

The basic concept for dealing with integers or other signed numbers involves the idea of opposites. Each integer has an opposite, as the examples below show.

Integer	Opposite
5	-5
-17	17

What happens if a number and its opposite are added together?

For example adding 1 and -1:

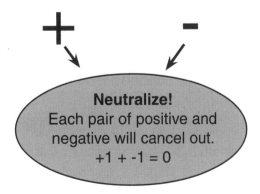

Neutralize!
Each pair of positive and negative will cancel out.
+1 + -1 = 0

35

Chapter 3: Working With Integers and Signed Numbers (cont.)

The sum of an integer and its opposite integer will always be zero! This result is true for all integers and is called the Additive Inverse Property of Addition.

For every integer, *a,* there is a unique integer, *-a* so that, $a + (-a) = 0$. The integer *-a* is called the **additive inverse** of *a.*

❹ Addition of Integers

Adding integers becomes a simple process if we put together basic addition facts and the new property just presented. To add numbers like 3 and -5, a model using +'s and –'s can be used. The illustration below shows three + signs representing the 3 and five – signs representing the -5. As stated above, adding one + and one – = 0, forming a neutral pair. Look for all the neutral pairs in the model below, pairing one + with one – to form 0 by the additive inverse property. What is left unpaired? In this example, two –'s are left unpaired.

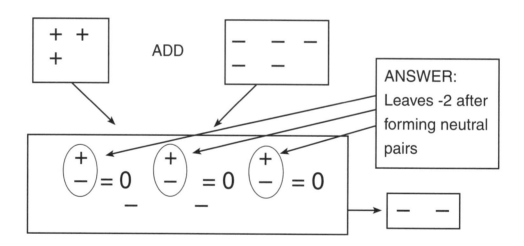

Example of Adding Two Integers With Different Signs:

Problem: -34 + 52 = ?

Step 1: Decide which of the addends will have more power or absolute value. This determines if the answer is positive or negative.

1. Which addend, -34 or 52, has more power? In this case, the positive 52 has more power than the negative 34, so the answer will be positive.

Chapter 3: Working With Integers and Signed Numbers (cont.)

Step 2: Find the difference in the absolute values of the two numbers (treating both as positive quantities).

   2. Find the difference between 52 and 34.

   3. 52 – 34 = 18.

Step 3: Take your answer from Step Two and attach the appropriate sign from Step One.

   4. In #1, we found that the answer would be positive. Add that sign to the answer.

   5. **Answer:**   So, -34 + 52 = 18.

Example of Adding Integers With the Same Signs:

Both Positive — Add as always and get a positive answer.

     Example: 17 + 76 = 93

Both Negative — Add as if they are both positive, and then attach a negative sign to your answer.

     Example: -17 + -76 = -93

5 Subtraction of Integers

When subtracting integers, connect what is known about subtraction of whole numbers, basic subtraction facts, and take advantage of patterns seen.

Subtracting Integers – Same Sign

Example of Subtracting Integers Both Positive:

    8 – 3 = ?

When subtracting two positive integers, think about what the symbols ask you to do. We need to start with eight +'s and from that set remove (subtract) three +'s and look to see what is left. We know that there are five +'s left. So, 8 – 3 = 5.

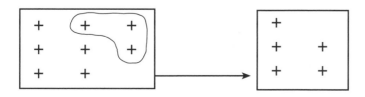

Chapter 3: Working With Integers and Signed Numbers (cont.)

Example of Subtracting Negative Integers:

-8 − -3 = ?

When subtracting two negative integers, think about what the symbols ask you to do. We need to start with a set that has eight −'s in it, and then remove (subtract) three −'s and look to see what is left. We know that there are five −'s left. So, -8 − -3 = -5

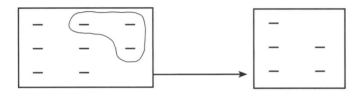

Subtracting Two Integers With Different Signs

Example of Subtracting Two Integers With One Positive and One Negative Sign:

-6 − 2 = ?

Look at the symbols, start with six −'s, and then from that set remove two +'s. If the set only has −'s, where do we get the +'s to remove? One solution is to put in some neutral pairs, + and −, to be able to remove the necessary two +'s. After removing the two +'s, what is the value of the set that is left? It shows eight −'s. So, -6 − 2 = -8.

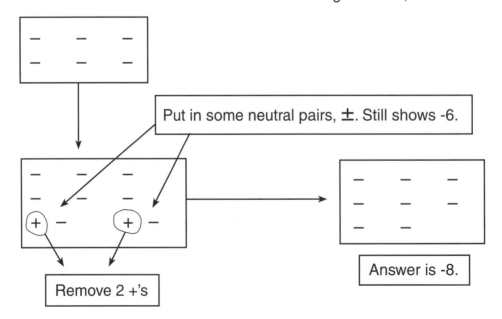

While the model used above will work in all situations, it would be helpful to find a more efficient way to compute subtraction problems.

Chapter 3: Working With Integers and Signed Numbers (cont.)

Look at the problems in the table below, and see if there is a pattern that would help work with subtraction of integers of opposite signs.

Subtraction Problem	Answer	Addition Problem	Answer
6 – 2	4	6 + -2	4
-5 – 3	-8	-5 + -3	-8
7 – -2	9	7 + 2	9
-3 – -7	4	-3 + 7	4
47 – 23	24	47 + -23	24

1. Compare the subtraction problem to its partner addition problem. Each problem has the same solution.
2. How do the problems differ? Let's look at the first pair of problems

Subtraction Problem	Answer	Addition Problem	Answer
6 – 2	4	6 + -2	4

- Both problems start with the same first number, 6.
- The two problems have different operations, subtraction versus addition.
- The subtraction problem has 2 as the second number. The addition problem has -2 (additive inverse of 2) as its second number.
- The answers are the same.

Does this pattern hold when comparing 47 – 23 = 24 and 47 + -23 = 24? Both of these problems have the same first number, 47. The problems have different operation signs, subtraction versus addition. In both problems, the second numbers are additive inverses or opposites, 23 and -23. Are the answers the same? Yes. This pattern allows the replacement of any integer subtraction problem with an equivalent integer addition problem.

Chapter 3: Working With Integers and Signed Numbers (cont.)

Integer Subtraction Rule

For all integers *a* and *b*

$$a - b = a + \text{-}b$$

Examples:

Problem: -6 – 15 = ?

Step 1: Think of the equivalent addition problem, -6 + -15 = ?

Step 2: Since the numbers have the same sign, add 6 and 15 to get 21 and attach the negative sign.

Step 3: Since -6 + -15 = -21, we know -6 – 15 = -21.

Answer: -6 – 15 = -21

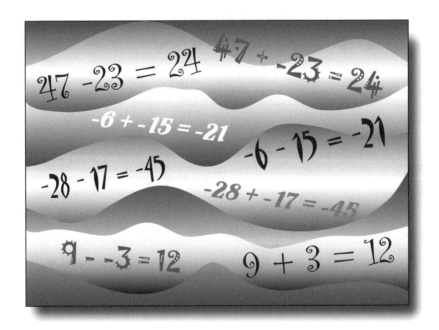

Name: _____ Date: _____

Practice: Integers and Signed Numbers— It's all just ADDITION!

Directions: Evaluate each of the following.

1. $5 - -3 =$ _____

2. $-17 + -9 =$ _____

3. $|0| =$ _____

4. $-24 + 56 =$ _____

5. $|-21| =$ _____

6. $15 - -8 =$ _____

7. $|73| =$ _____

8. $45 + -19 =$ _____

9. $|-7 + -3| =$ _____

10. $|2 - -13| =$ _____

Chapter 3: Working With Integers and Signed Numbers (cont.)

6 Multiplication of Integers

Multiplication of integers uses what you already know about multiplication of whole numbers. Consider the problem 3 x 5. One way to think about 3 x 5, is as three groups with five objects in each group. So, multiplying two positive integers results in a positive integer answer, 3 x 5 = 15.

Multiplying Two Integers With Different Signs (one positive, one negative)

Using the same thinking with the multiplication problem, 3 x -5, there would be three groups with five negatives in each. The figure then would show that the final answer is -5 + -5 + -5 = -15, or using multiplication, 3 x -5 = -15.

-5   +   -5   +   -5   =   -15

Rule for multiplying two integers with different signs:

Multiply as if both were positive, and make the final answer negative.

Multiplying Two Negative Integers

Use what we know at this point about multiplying integers to investigate what the answer to -3 x -5 must be to work with the previous rules. Consider the table below, and look at the way the answers change—is there a pattern that sets up the obvious answer for -3 x -5?

3 x -5 = -15	Solution is in the illustration above.
2 x -5 = -10	Apply the different sign rule for multiplication.
1 x -5 = -5	Identity Property – any number multiplied by one is the number.
0 x -5 = 0	Zero Property – any number multiplied by zero is zero.
-1 x -5 = 5	Look at the pattern of answers, each changed by adding 5 to the previous answer, -15 + 5 = -10, -10 + 5 = -5, so -1 x -5 must = 5.
-2 x -5 = 10	Follow the pattern.
-3 x -5 = 15	Note that the answer is positive, that -3 x -5 = 3 x 5 = 15.

Chapter 3: Working With Integers and Signed Numbers (cont.)

Rule for multiplying two negative integers:
Multiply as if both were positive, and make the final answer positive.

7 **Division of Integers**

Learning division is simply a matter of connecting division to multiplication. Since division and multiplication are inverse operations, integer division is built on what we already know. To answer the division problem, $15 \div 3$, most of us think of the associated multiplication problem, 3 x what number = 15, and know that 5 is the solution.

The same thinking holds for integer division. Let's consider $-15 \div 3$ and outline the thinking process used to find the answer.

Find: $-15 \div 3 = ?$

Step 1: Think: 3 x what number = -15

Step 2: Know the basic fact: 3 x 5 = 15

Step 3: We want to end up with -15, not 15. We know the first factor, 3, is positive, so if -5 is the second factor, 3 x -5 = -15. A positive times a negative yields a negative answer.

Step 4: Found: $-15 \div 3 = -5$

This connection between multiplication and division allows us to "coast" using multiplication knowledge to find division answers.

$-24 \div 6 = ?$ $6 \times ? = -24$ -4

$30 \div -2 = ?$ $-2 \times ? = 30$ -15

$-48 \div -12 = ?$ $-12 \times ? = -48$ 4

43

Name: _____ Date: _____

Practice: Coasting Between Multiplication and Division

Directions: Solve the following problems.

1. -7 x 3 = _____

2. 20 x -5 = _____

3. 0 ÷ 7 = _____

4. 100 ÷ -10 = _____

5. 11 x -3 = _____

6. -36 ÷ 6 = _____

7. -2 x -8 = _____

8. -72 ÷ -6 = _____

9. -3(6 + -2) = _____

10. 12 ÷ -6 + 4 − -7 = _____

Chapter 3: Working With Integers and Signed Numbers (cont.)

8 Operating on Signed Numbers

The first part of this section has focused on the set of integers, {…, -3, -2, -1, 0, 1, 2, 3, …}, and how to add, subtract, multiply, and divide these types of numbers. There are other negative and positive numbers that are not integers.

Examples of Positive and Negative Numbers That are Not Integers:

$$-\frac{1}{2} \qquad 0.76 \qquad -21.35 \qquad 4\frac{3}{4} \qquad -\sqrt{2}$$

Another way to ask the question is, how do I add, subtract, multiply, and divide real numbers, knowing that some are positive and some are negative? Every real number except 0 has a sign attached to it. We just use the results that work for integers.

For example, $\dfrac{\cancel{5}}{7} \times -\dfrac{3}{\cancel{10}} = \dfrac{1}{7} \times -\dfrac{3}{2} = -\dfrac{3}{14}$

Solving this problem:

A positive multiplied by a negative gives a negative answer.

Multiply fractions as usual, simplifying any common factors.

Example: 21.7 + -10.3 = 11.4

Step 1: Since the addends differ in sign, find the difference.
$$21.7 - 10.3 = 11.4$$

Step 2: Take the answer as positive, since |21.7| is bigger than |-10.3|.

In short, all earlier rules for sign still hold. Practice putting them into action with a variety of signed real numbers and the indicated operations.

Name: _____ Date: _____

Chapter 3: Working With Integers and Signed Numbers (cont.)

Practice: All Numbers, All Signs, Let's Operate!

Directions: Solve the following problems.

1. $-\frac{3}{5} \times \frac{7}{8} =$ _____

2. $7.8 + -5.3 =$ _____

3. $-110 \div 2.5 =$ _____

4. $5\sqrt{3} + -11\sqrt{3} =$ _____

5. $-2.3 \times -10.2 =$ _____

6. $5 \times -36 =$ _____

7. $-\frac{2}{3} + \frac{5}{6} =$ _____

8. $-\frac{10}{11} \div \frac{15}{22} =$ _____

9. $2(4.7 + -3.6) =$ _____

10. $|-7 - -3.5| =$ _____

Name: _____ Date: _____

Practice: Integers and Signed Numbers

Directions: Evaluate each of the following.

1. -33 + -9 = _____

2. -24 + 56 = _____

3. |-33| = _____

4. 15 – -8 = _____

5. |88| = _____

6. |-8 + -35| = _____

7. |2 – -13| = _____

8. -5 x 15 = _____

9. -3 x -9 = _____

10. -432 ÷ -6 = _____

11. -3(8 + -3) = _____

12. 24 ÷ -6 + 4 – -7 = _____

13. $-\frac{3}{7} \times \frac{7}{8}$ = _____

14. $6\sqrt{5} + -11\sqrt{5}$ = _____

15. $-\frac{10}{13} \div \frac{16}{26}$ = _____

16. |-9 – -3.5| = _____

47

Chapter 3: Working With Integers and Signed Numbers (cont.)

Summary of Integers and Signed Numbers

- We define the set of integers as {…, -3, -2, -1, 0, 1, 2, 3, …}.
- Additive Inverse Property of Addition: Every real number, a, has a unique opposite, $-a$, so that, $a + (-a) = 0$. The real number $-a$ is called the additive inverse of a.
- Adding Signed Numbers (integers or other real numbers):
  - Both Positive – Add as always and get a positive answer.
  - Both Negative – Add as if both positive and attach a negative sign to the answer.
  - Differing in Sign – Find the difference in the absolute values of the two numbers and attach the sign of the addend with the largest absolute value.
- Subtracting Signed Numbers: Use the Signed Number Subtraction Rule, change $a - b$ to $a + -b$.
- Multiplying Signed Numbers:

Sign of 1st factor	Sign of 2nd factor	Sign of product/answer
+	+	+
−	+	−
+	−	−
−	−	+

- Division of Signed Numbers: Think multiplication and use what you know!

Tips to Remember

It's all about using the inverse. Change subtraction to addition and division to multiplication!

-4 – 5 = ?	Think: -4 + -5 = ?
-20 ÷ 5 = ?	Think: 5 x what = -20

Real Life Applications of Integers and Signed Numbers

Integers and signed numbers are used in describing temperatures, reporting golf scores (below par, even, over par), accounting, and in reporting the fluctuations in the stock market (up $1\frac{1}{4}$ or down -2).

Chapter 4: Properties of Numbers

Introduction to the Concepts of Properties of Numbers

Numbers operations have certain properties or rules. The properties related to algebra include the Identity Properties, Commutative Properties, and Associative Properties of addition and multiplication and the Distributive Property of multiplication over addition.

Concepts of Properties of Numbers

1 Identity Property of Addition

2 Identity Property of Multiplication

3 Commutative Property of Addition

4 Commutative Property of Multiplication

5 Associative Property of Addition

6 Associative Property of Multiplication

7 Inverse Operations

8 Reciprocal or Multiplicative Inverse Operations

9 Distributive Property of Multiplication Over Addition

Explanations of Concepts of Properties of Numbers

1   **Identity Property of Addition**

When adding or subtracting zero to or from any number or variable, the answer is the number or variable.

Examples of adding or subtracting zero to numbers or variables:

If you have three apples and you add zero apples, how many do you have?

   + 0 apples =

$4 + 0 = 4$

$a + 0 = a$

$2b + 0 = 2b$

Chapter 4: Properties of Numbers (cont.)

2 **Identity Property of Multiplication**

The Identity Property of Multiplication states that any number or variable multiplied by 1 is that number or variable.

Examples of the Identity Property of Multiplication:

$13 \times 1 = 13$ $1 \times 13 = 13$

$c \cdot 1 = c$ $1 \cdot c = c$

3 **Commutative Property of Addition**

The Commutative Property of Addition states that it does not matter in what order you add numbers. The sum is always the same.

Examples of the Commutative Property of Addition:

$5 + 6 = 6 + 5$
$5 + 6 = 11$ and $6 + 5 = 11$
Therefore, $5 + 6 = 6 + 5$ because $11 = 11$

$4 + 6 + 7 = 7 + 4 + 6$
       $17 = 17$

$a + b + c = b + a + c$

4 **Commutative Property of Multiplication**

The Commutative Property of Multiplication states that no matter in what order you multiply two numbers, the answer is always the same.

Examples of the Commutative Property of Multiplication:

$3 \times 8 = 8 \times 3$
$3 \times 8 = 24$ and $8 \times 3 = 24$
   $24 = 24$
Therefore, $3 \times 8 = 8 \times 3$

Chapter 4: Properties of Numbers (cont.)

$$20 \times \tfrac{1}{2} = \tfrac{1}{2} \times 20$$

$$20 \times \tfrac{1}{2} = 10 \text{ and } \tfrac{1}{2} \times 20 = 10$$
$$10 = 10$$

Therefore, $20 \times \tfrac{1}{2} = \tfrac{1}{2} \times 20$

5 Associative Property of Addition

The Associative Property of Addition states that when you add three numbers together, the sum will be the same no matter how you group them.

Examples of the Associative Property of Addition:

$(5 + 6) + 7 = 5 + (6 + 7)$

Step 1: Remember, you add the numbers in parentheses first.

$(5 + 6) = 11$ $(6 + 7) = 13$

Step 2: Then add the sum and the remaining number on both sides.

$11 + 7 = 18$ $5 + 13 = 18$

$18 = 18$

Therefore, $(5 + 6) + 7 = 5 + (6 + 7)$

$7 + (9 + 10) = (7 + 9) + 10$

Step 1: Remember, you add the numbers in parentheses first.

$(9 + 10) = 19$ $(7 + 9) = 16$

Step 2: Then add the sum and the remaining number on both sides.

$7 + 19 = 26$ $16 + 10 = 26$

$26 = 26$

Therefore, $7 + (9 + 10) = (7 + 9) + 10$

Chapter 4: Properties of Numbers (cont.)

6 Associative Property of Multiplication

The Associative Property of Multiplication states that when you multiply three numbers together, the answer will always be the same no matter how you group them.

Examples of the Associative Property of Multiplication:

$(5 \times 4) \times 8 = 5 \times (4 \times 8)$

Step 1: Remember, you multiply numbers in parentheses first.

$(5 \times 4) = 20$ $(4 \times 8) = 32$

Step 2: Then multiply what was in the parentheses and the remaining number on both sides.

$20 \times 8 = 160$ $5 \times 32 = 160$

$160 = 160$

Therefore, $(5 \times 4) \times 8 = 5 \times (4 \times 8)$

$(10 \times 4) \times 5 = 10 \times (4 \times 5)$

Step 1: Remember, you multiply numbers in parentheses first.

$(10 \times 4) = 40$ $(4 \times 5) = 20$

Step 2: Then multiply what was in the parentheses and the remaining number on both sides.

$40 \times 5 = 200$ $10 \times 20 = 200$

$200 = 200$

Therefore, $(10 \times 4) \times 5 = 10 \times (4 \times 5)$

$(a \bullet b) \bullet c = a \bullet (b \bullet c)$

Step 1: Remember, you multiply numbers in parentheses first.

$(a \bullet b) = ab$ $(b \bullet c) = bc$

Step 2: Then multiply what was in the parentheses and the remaining number on both sides.

$ab \bullet c = abc$ $a \bullet bc = abc$

$abc = abc$

Therefore, $(a \bullet b) \bullet c = a \bullet (b \bullet c)$

Chapter 4: Properties of Numbers (cont.)

7 Inverse Operations

Inverse Operations are operations that cancel each other. For example, addition and subtraction are inverse operations. Multiplication and division are inverse operations.

Examples of Inverse Operations:

$5n - 9$

If you add 9, it undoes subtracting the 9, and you end up with $5n$ again.

$9 - 9 = 0$

The addition undoes the subtraction.

$7 \bullet n = 7n$

If you divide $7n$ by 7, you undo the multiplication.

$$\frac{7n}{7} = \frac{7}{7} = 1 \text{ so } 1 \bullet n = n$$

The division undoes the multiplication.

8 Reciprocal or Multiplicative Inverse Operations

Reciprocal or Multiplicative Inverse Operations are operations in which two numbers are multiplied and the product is 1.

For any non-zero number:

$$\text{Number} \times \frac{1}{\text{Number}} = 1 \qquad \frac{1}{\text{Number}} \times \text{Number} = 1$$

Examples of Reciprocal or Multiplicative Inverse Operations:

5 and $\frac{1}{5}$ are reciprocal

$5 \times \frac{1}{5} =$ $\qquad\qquad$ $\frac{5}{1} \times \frac{1}{5} = \frac{5}{5} = 1$ $\qquad$ $5 \times \frac{1}{5} = 1$

Therefore, 5 and $\frac{1}{5}$ are reciprocal because when they are multiplied together, they equal 1.

Chapter 4: Properties of Numbers (cont.)

$\frac{3}{4}$ is the reciprocal of $1\frac{1}{3}$.

$$1\frac{1}{3} = \frac{4}{3}$$

$\frac{3}{4}$ is the reciprocal of $\frac{4}{3}$.

$$\frac{3}{4} \times \frac{4}{3} = \frac{3 \times 4}{4 \times 3} = \frac{12}{12} = 1$$

Therefore, $\frac{3}{4}$ is reciprocal of $1\frac{1}{3}$.

1 is its own reciprocal.

$1 \times 1 = 1$

-1 is its own reciprocal.

$-1 \times -1 = 1$

When you multiply two negative numbers, you end up with a positive number as the product.

-1 is its own reciprocal.

0 has no reciprocal.

0 times any number is 0.

Chapter 4: Properties of Numbers (cont.)

9 Distributive Property of Multiplication Over Addition

This property is most generally called the Distributive Property. The basic rule uncovered here is that when you have both the operation of addition and the operation of multiplication to do, you can decide which you want to do first. Suppose you have 3(2 + 5) to simplify. Notice that you have addition in the parentheses, and then you need to multiply by 3. So by order of operations, $3(2 + 5) = 3(7) = 21$. But we could do the multiplication first, as long as we distribute. What does this mean? Think about an arrow that links 3 to each part of the addition problem.

$$3(2 + 5) = 3 \times 2 + 3 \times 5 = 6 + 15 = 21$$

Notice that this answer, when we distribute, multiply first, and then add, is the same as our first answer.

In general, $a(b + c) = a \cdot b + a \cdot c$ for any real numbers.

Examples Using the Distributive Property:

$3(x + 7) = 3 \cdot x + 3 \cdot 7 = 3x + 21$

$b(b + 1) = b \cdot b + b \cdot 1 = b^2 + b$

Name: _____ Date: _____

Chapter 4: Properties of Numbers (cont.)

Practice: Properties of Numbers

Directions: Solve the problems below and identify which property or properties the problem represents.

Identity Property of Addition   **Identity Property of Multiplication**
Commutative Property of Addition   **Commutative Property of Multiplication**
Associative Property of Addition   **Associative Property of Multiplication**
Inverse Operations   **Distributive Property**
Reciprocal or Multiplicative Inverse Operations

	Simplify	Property
1. $6 + 0 =$	_____	_____
2. $0 + c =$	_____	_____
3. $2b + 0 =$	_____	_____
4. $8 \times 1 =$	_____	_____
5. $1 \times 350 =$	_____	_____
6. $b \cdot 1 =$	_____	_____
7. $3 + 7 = 7 + 3$	_____	_____
8. $\frac{1}{5} \times 1 =$	_____	_____
9. $\frac{1}{5} \times 0 = 0 \times \frac{1}{5}$	_____	_____
10. $3y \cdot 7 = 7 \cdot 3y$	_____	_____
11. $a + b = b + a$	_____	_____

Name: _____ Date: _____

Chapter 4: Properties of Numbers (cont.)

	Simplify	**Property**

12. $7 \times 9 = 9 \times 7$ _____ _____

13. $(3 + 9) + 7 = 3 + (9 + 7)$ _____ _____

14. $\dfrac{5x}{5} =$ _____ _____

15. $(3 \times 4) \times 8 = 3 \times (4 \times 8)$ _____ _____

16. $(d \bullet b) \bullet c = d \bullet (b \bullet c)$ _____ _____

17. $x - 7 + 7 =$ _____ _____

18. $5 - 6 + 6 =$ _____ _____

19. $3(5 + 2) = 3 \times 5 + 3 \times 2$ _____ _____

20. $a(b + c) = a \bullet b + a \bullet c$ _____ _____

21. $a \bullet \dfrac{1}{a} =$ _____ _____

Name: _____ Date: _____

Chapter 4: Properties of Numbers (cont.)

Practice: Whose Property Is It?

Directions: Match the examples below in the second column with the correct property in the first column.

_____ 1. Identity Property of Addition

A. $5(33 + 2) = 5 \times 33 + 5 \times 2$

_____ 2. Identity Property of Multiplication

B. $5 \times 33 = 33 \times 5$

_____ 3. Commutative Property of Addition

C. $(5 \times 33) \times 2 = 5 \times (33 \times 2)$

_____ 4. Commutative Property of Multiplication

D. $33 \times 1 = 33$

_____ 5. Associative Property of Addition

E. $55 + 0 = 55$

_____ 6. Associative Property of Multiplication

F. $5 + 35 + 2 = 2 + 35 + 5$

_____ 7. Inverse Operations

G. $5 \times \frac{1}{5} = 1$

_____ 8. Reciprocal or Multiplicative Inverse Operations

H. Addition and Subtraction/ Multiplication and Division

_____ 9. Distributive Properties

I. $(5 + 33) + 2 = 5 + (33 + 2)$

Directions: Answer the following questions.

10. What is the identity number for addition and subtraction? _____

11. Why is the number in question 10 called an identity number for addition and subtraction?

_____

_____

12. What is the identity number for multiplication? _____

13. Why is the number in question 12 called the identity number for multiplication?

_____

_____

14. Why are addition and subtraction and multiplication and division called reciprocal or inverse operations?

_____

_____

Chapter 4: Properties of Numbers (cont.)

Summary of Properties of Numbers

Number operations have certain properties or rules. The properties related to algebra include the Identity Properties, Commutative Properties, and Associative Properties of addition and multiplication and the Distributive Property of multiplication over addition.

Identity Property of Addition	$a + 0 = a$
Identity Property of Multiplication	$b \cdot 1 = b$
Commutative Property of Addition	$a + b + c = c + b + a$
Commutative Property of Multiplication	$a \cdot b = b \cdot a$
Associative Property of Addition	$(a + b) + c = a + (b + c)$
Associative Property of Multiplication	$(a \cdot b) \cdot c = a \cdot (b \cdot c)$
Inverse Operations	Addition and Subtraction Multiplication and Division
Reciprocal or Multiplicative Inverse Operations	$a \cdot \dfrac{1}{a} = 1$
Distributive Property	$a(b + c) = a \cdot b + a \cdot c$

Tips to Remember

Zero plus any number is that number, so it identifies the original number.
$$2{,}567 + 0 = 2{,}567 \qquad a + 0 = a$$
Any number multiplied by one identifies the original number.
$$45{,}987 \times 1 = 45{,}987 \qquad c \cdot 1 = c$$
Addition and multiplication have commutative properties because it does not matter in what order you add or multiply the numbers. In division, the order of numbers makes a difference in the answers, so division does not have a commutative property.

Addition and multiplication have associative properties because it does not matter how you group the numbers. The answer is the same.

To demostrate the distributive property of multiplication over addition in expressions such as $4(a + 5a)$, multiply and then add.

Real Life Applications of Properties of Numbers

Properties of numbers are used in accounting, finding velocity, chemistry, finding profits, finding times in different time zones, and art.

Chapter 5: Exponents and Exponential Expressions

Introduction to Exponents and Exponential Expressions

Many times in working with mathematics, we need to multiply the same number by itself many times. For example, when bacteria double each hour, to think about how many bacteria you have after 13 hours—starting with one bacteria—you need to find:

2 x 2 x 2 x 2 x 2 x 2 x 2 x 2 x 2 x 2 x 2 x 2 x 2

Rather than have to write out the repeated multiplication, symbols called **exponents** can be used as shorthand notation to indicate the action of repeated multiplication. The repeated multiplication above can be written as 2^{13}. In this section, we will be looking at how exponents are used, how to evaluate expressions using exponents, and discovering what rules are helpful in simplifying and evaluating exponent expressions.

Concepts of Exponents and Exponential Expressions

❶ Exponents or Powers

❷ Scientific Notation

❸ Exponential Expressions

❹ Rules for Whole Number Exponents

   Ⓐ Multiplication Rule

   Ⓑ Dividing Expressions With the Same Base

   Ⓒ Division Rule

   Ⓓ Negative Exponents

   Ⓔ Dividing Exponential Expressions

   Ⓕ Raising to the Zero Power

   Ⓖ Raising a Power to a Power

   Ⓗ Power to a Power Rule

   Ⓘ Evaluating Exponential Expressions

   Ⓙ Adding and Subtracting Exponential Expressions With Coefficients

Chapter 5: Exponents and Exponential Expressions (cont.)

Explanations of the Concepts of Exponents and Exponential Expressions

1 **Exponents or Powers**

The **exponent** is the number indicating how many times the number is multiplied by itself. The **square** of a number means you multiply the number by itself. The **cube** of a number means you multiply the number times itself three times. In the exponential expression 4^3, the 4 is the root and the ^{3} is the exponent. 4^3 is the same as 4 x 4 x 4. Since there are no parentheses, start at the left and move right 4 x 4 = 16, 16 x 4 = 64, so 4^3 = 64.

Examples of Exponents:

The square of a number means you multiply the number by itself. For example, 7^2 means 7 squared or 7 raised to the second power.

7 x 7 = 49

So 7^2 = 49

2 **Scientific Notation**

Scientists use exponents in scientific notation when they are working with very large or very small numbers.

Example:

10^8 = 10 to the eighth power

this is 10 times itself 8 times or 10 x 10 x 10 x 10 x 10 x 10 x 10 x 10 = 100,000,000

10^8 = 100,000,000

3 **Exponential Expressions**

Exponents are sometimes used in a combination of numbers and variables together, and these are called **algebraic expressions**. For example, $3x^5$, $(5x^3y)^4$, and $(4 + x)^2$ are examples of algebraic expressions that use exponents. Many times, we need to simplify these expressions as a part of solving equations and problems. To help in simplification, there are some simple rules that are useful.

Chapter 5: Exponents and Exponential Expressions (cont.)

④ Rules for Whole Number Exponents

Ⓐ Multiplication Rule

In general, $a^m \cdot a^n = a^{m+n}$. In words, if you are multiplying exponential expressions with the same base, add the exponents and keep the same base.

Example of Multiplying Exponential Expressions With Coefficients:

Problem: $(3x^2)(5x^5) =$

Step 1: Multiply the coefficients. $(3)(5) = 15$

Step 2: Add the exponents. $2 + 5 = 7$

Step 3: Combine the terms.

Answer: $15x^7$

Ⓑ Dividing Expressions With the Same Base

Example: Suppose we need to simplify the expression, $a^5 \div a^2$

To investigate, let's think of the division in fraction form, $\dfrac{a^5}{a^2}$

This should be simple to do using the definition of exponent.

What does a^5 mean? $a \cdot a \cdot a \cdot a \cdot a$

What does a^2 mean? $a \cdot a$

That means that $\dfrac{a^5}{a^2} = \dfrac{a \cdot a \cdot a \cdot \cancel{a} \cdot \cancel{a}}{\cancel{a} \cdot \cancel{a}} = a \cdot a \cdot a = a^3$

Consider the exponents 5 and 2. What was the new simplified exponent? 3.
How do we get 3 from 5 and 2? SUBTRACT.

Chapter 5: Exponents and Exponential Expressions (cont.)

Ⓒ Division Rule

In general, $a^m \div a^n = a^{m-n}$. In words, if you are dividing exponential expressions with the same base, subtract the exponents and keep the same base.

Examples of Dividing Exponential Expressions:

Problem: $8^5 \div 8^2 =$

Step 1: Subtract the exponents. $5 - 2 = 3$

Answer: $8^5 \div 8^2 = 8^3$ or 512

Problem: $\dfrac{6x^2}{6x^3}$

Step 1: Subtract the exponents. x^{2-3}

Answer: Note that $6 \div 6 = 1$, so x^{-1} is the simplified answer.

Problem: $x^4 \div x^{(-4)}$

Step 1: Subtract the exponents. $4 - (-4) = 8$

Answer: $x^4 \div x^{(-4)} = x^8$

Problem: $8b^4 \div 2b^2$

Step 1: Divide the coefficients. $8 \div 2 = 4$

Step 2: Subtract the exponents. $4 - 2 = 2$

Answer: $8b^4 \div 2b^2 = 4b^2$

Problem: $b^{-4} \div b^{-2}$

Step 1: Subtract the exponents. $(-4) - (-2) = -2$

Answer: $b^{-4} \div b^{-2} = b^{-2}$

In the last example, the base is raised to a negative exponent. How should this be interpreted? As b times itself negative 2 times? We will answer that in the next section.

Chapter 5: Exponents and Exponential Expressions (cont.)

D   **Negative Exponents**

To solve problems with negative exponents, find the reciprocal of a number. When you find the **reciprocal** of a number, you make the numerator the denominator and the denominator the numerator.

Examples of Reciprocals:

$\frac{1}{2}$ reciprocal is $\frac{2}{1}$ 3 reciprocal is $\frac{1}{3}$ $\frac{a}{b}$ reciprocal is $\frac{b}{a}$

Change the negative exponents to reciprocals by taking the reciprocal of the base number and changing the exponent to a positive number.

Examples of Solving Problems With Negative Exponents:

Problem: 5^{-2}

Step 1: Find the reciprocal of the base number.

$5 = \frac{5}{1}$ The reciprocal is $\frac{1}{5}$.

Step 2: Change the exponent in the reciprocal to a positive number. $\frac{1}{5^2}$

Answer: $5^{-2} = \frac{1}{5^2} = \frac{1}{25}$

Problem: x^{-4}

Step 1: Find the reciprocal of the base number.

$x = \frac{x}{1}$ The reciprocal is $\frac{1}{x}$.

Step 2: Change the exponent in the reciprocal to a positive number. $\frac{1}{x^4}$

Answer: $x^{-4} = \frac{1}{x^4}$

Chapter 5: Exponents and Exponential Expressions (cont.)

E **Dividing Exponential Expressions**

To divide exponential expressions with the same root or base, subtract the exponents and put the answer with the root or base number. For example, in $4^5 \div 4^2$, the root or base is 4, and the exponents are ^{5} and ^{2}. Subtract the exponents $^{5-2=3.}$ Put the answer with the root 4, so $4^5 \div 4^2 = 4^3$. You can divide exponential expressions with coefficients, if they have the same base or root. Divide the coefficients, subtract the exponents, and combine the terms. For example, in $4d^6 \div 2d^2$ the exponents are ^{6} and ^{2}. Subtract the exponents $^{6-2=4.}$ Divide the coefficients $4 \div 2 = 2$. Put the answers for the exponent and the coefficients with the root $2d^4$. So $4d^6 \div 2d^2 = 2d^4$.

Examples of Dividing Exponential Expressions:

Problem: $8^5 \div 8^2 =$

Step 1: Subtract the exponents. $^{5-2=3}$

Answer: $8^5 \div 8^2 = 8^3$ or 512

Problem: $\dfrac{6x^2}{6x^3}$ **Step 1:** $6 \div 6 = 1$

Step 2: Subtract the exponents. $^{2-3=-1}$

Answer: x^{-1} or $\dfrac{1}{x}$

Problem: $x^4 \div x^{(-4)}$

Step 1: Subtract the exponents. $^{4-(-4)=8}$

Answer: $x^4 \div x^{(-4)} = x^8$

Problem: $b^{-4} \div b^{-2}$

Step 1: Subtract the exponents. $^{(-4)-(-2)=-2}$

Answer: $b^{-4} \div b^{-2} = b^{-2}$

Problem: $8b^4 \div 2b^2$

Step 1: Divide the coefficients. $8 \div 2 = 4$

Step 2: Subtract the exponents. $^{4-2=2}$

Answer: $8b^4 \div 2b^2 = 4b^2$

DIVIDING EXPONENTIAL EXPRESSIONS

Chapter 5: Exponents and Exponential Expressions (cont.)

(F)   Raising to the Zero Power

If we can have any number as an exponent, what does 2^0 mean? Let's try to use our earlier understanding to see what the answer should be. Suppose we start with $\frac{2^4}{2^4}$. We know that any number divided by itself is 1. So, we know that $\frac{2^4}{2^4} = 1$. But the rule for dividing exponential expressions with the same base says you simplify by subtracting exponents to get the new exponent. That would mean that $\frac{2^4}{2^4} = 2^{4-4} = 2^0$. This tells us that $\frac{2^4}{2^4} = 1$ and $\frac{2^4}{2^4} = 2^0$. This has to mean that $2^0 = 1$.

In general, $a^0 = 1$. In words, any base raised to the zero power is 1.

(G)   Raising a Power to a Power

Consider how to handle $(3^3)^2$. We want to raise a power to another power. If the definition of exponent is used, we can investigate how this should work. Consider the meaning of 3^3. $3^3 = 3 \times 3 \times 3$. This gives the result that $(3^3)^2 = (3 \times 3 \times 3)^2$. Raising the inside to the second power would mean to take what is inside the parentheses and multiply it by itself so $(3^3)^2 = (3 \times 3 \times 3)^2 = (3 \times 3 \times 3)(3 \times 3 \times 3) = 3 \times 3 \times 3 \times 3 \times 3 \times 3 = 3^6$. Consider the exponents 3 and 2. What was the new simplified exponent? 6. How do we get 6 from 3 and 2? MULTIPLY.

(H)   Power to a Power Rule

In general, $(a^m)^n = a^{m \cdot n}$. In words, to raise a power to a power, multiply the exponents.

Examples of Raising the Exponential Power:

Problem: $(2^2)^5$

Step 1: Multiply the exponents. $2 \times 5 = 10$

Step 2: Raise the number to the power. $(2^2)^5 = 2^{10} = 1{,}024$

Answer: $(2^2)^5 = 1{,}024$

Chapter 5: Exponents and Exponential Expressions (cont.)

Problem: $(5^5)^0$

Step 1: Multiply the exponents. $5 \times 0 = 0$

Step 2: Remember 0 times any number is 0. (Any number to the zero power is 1.)

Answer: $(5^5)^0 = 5^0 = 1$

Ⓘ   **Evaluating Exponential Expressions**

To evaluate exponential expressions, compute the value of the exponential expression as it falls according to the order of operations rules.

Examples of Multiplying Exponential Expressions With Coefficients:

Problem: $4(5)^2$

Step 1: First compute the value of the exponential expression.

$(5)^2 = (5 \times 5) = 25$

Step 2: Then multiply by the coefficient.

$4(25)$

Answer: Therefore, $4(5)^2 = 100$.

Problem: $6(7 - 3)^2 =$

Step 1: First do what is in the parentheses.

$7 - 3 = 4$

$6(4)^2 =$

Step 2: Compute the value of the exponential expression.

$6(4 \times 4) = 6(16)$

Step 3: Then multiply by the coefficient.

$6(16) = 96$

Answer: Therefore, $6(7 - 3)^2 = 96$.

Chapter 5: Exponents and Exponential Expressions (cont.)

J   **Adding and Subtracting Exponential Expressions With Coefficients**

Exponential expressions can be added or subtracted if they have exactly the same base and exactly the same exponent by adding or subtracting the coefficients. When the variable parts match exactly, we call these **like terms**.

Examples of Adding and Subtracting Exponential Expressions With Coefficients:

Problem: $4(y^3) + 8(y^3)$

The bases are exactly the same (the variable y and the exponent ^{3} are exactly the same), so the like terms can be added. Notice how this is like adding 4 apples + 8 apples. Add the coefficients. $4 + 8 = 12$

Answer: $4(y^3) + 8(y^3) = 12y^3$

Problem: $8(v^7) - 4(v^7)$

The bases are the same (the variable v and the exponent ^{7} are the same), so they can be subtracted.
Subtract the coefficients. $8 - 4 = 4$

Answer: $8(v^7) - 4(v^7) = 4v^7$

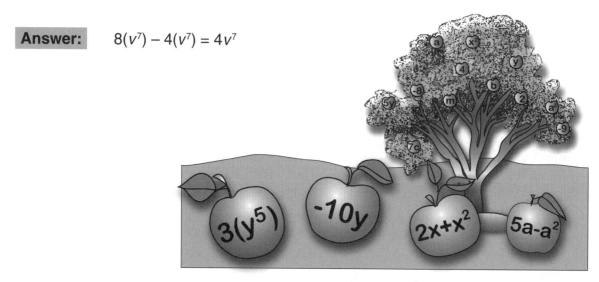

Name: _____ Date: _____

Chapter 5: Exponents and Exponential Expressions (cont.)

Practice: Exponents and Exponential Expressions

Directions: Solve and show your work.

Evaluate each exponential expression.

1. 10^2 _____

2. 5^5 _____

3. 6^{10} _____

4. 100^0 _____

5. y^0 _____

Evaluate exponential expressions with coefficients.

6. $3(5)^2$ _____

7. $5(-3)^3$ _____

8. $10(b)^2$ _____

Add and subtract with like terms.

9. $10(z^3) + 2(z^3)$ _____

10. $2(4^3) + (4^3)$ _____

11. $5(z^3) - 3(z^3)$ _____

12. $7(2^3) - 3(2^3)$ _____

13. $3(z^3) - 1(z)$ _____

Name: _____ Date: _____

Chapter 5: Exponents and Exponential Expressions (cont.)

Multiply exponential expressions.

14. $(z^3)(z^4)$ _____

15. $(a^3)(a^2)$ _____

Divide exponential expressions.

16. $3^2 \div 3$ _____

17. $x^4 \div x^2$ _____

18. $\dfrac{5^2}{1^3}$ _____

19. $\dfrac{4x^5}{2x^2}$ _____

Raise to the power.

20. $(3^5)^2$ _____

21. $(7^2)^0$ _____

22. $(2^2)^2$ _____

23. $(x^4)^2$ _____

Change the negative exponents to positive exponents.

24. 5^{-4} _____

25. 2^{-6} _____

26. $\left(\dfrac{1}{a}\right)^{-3}$ _____

Name: _____   Date: _____

Chapter 5: Exponents and Exponential Expressions (cont.)

Practice: Exponent Power!

Directions: Complete the exercises below as indicated.

What is my power?

_____ **1.** $5 \times 5 \times 5 \times 5 \times 5 \times 5 \times 5$

_____ **2.** $10 \times 10 \times 10 \times 10 \times 10 \times 10 \times 10 \times 10 \times 10 \times 10 \times 10 \times 10 \times 10 \times 10$

_____ **3.** $a \cdot a \cdot a \cdot a \cdot a \cdot a \cdot a \cdot a \cdot a \cdot a \cdot a \cdot a \cdot a \cdot a \cdot a \cdot a \cdot a \cdot a \cdot a$

Write what each of these represents in the long form.

4. 25^5 _____

5. b^{22} _____

6. $3c^5$ _____

7. $5d^3y$ _____

Find the actual number each represents.

8. 25^5 _____   **9.** 10^{10} _____

10. 8^7 _____   **11.** 35^6 _____

12. Why do scientists and mathematicians use exponents or raise numbers to a power?

_____

_____

Multiply the exponential expressions.

13. $(5x^2)(7x^5)$ _____

14. $a^5 \cdot a^8$ _____

15. $(3x^2)(2x^5)$ _____

16. $(9b^4)(2b^6)$ _____

Name: _____ Date: _____

Chapter 5: Exponents and Exponential Expressions (cont.)

Divide the exponential expressions.

17. $8^4 \div 8^2$ _____

18. $5^5 \div 5^2$ _____

19. $8b^4 \div 4b^2$ _____

20. $20c^6 \div 5c^3$ _____

Raise to the power indicated.

21. 5^0 _____

22. x^0 _____

23. $(3^3)^5$ _____

24. $(x^6)^2$ _____

25. $(4^2)^4$ _____

Evaluate the exponential expressions.

26. $5(3)^3$ _____

27. $3(6-2)^3$ _____

28. $4x^3 + 6x^3$ _____

29. $6^{-3} + 7^0$ _____

30. $7n^4 - 2n^4$ _____

Chapter 5: Exponents and Exponential Expressions (cont.)

Summary of Exponents and Exponential Expressions

The exponent is the number indicating how many times the number is multiplied by itself. The square of a number means you multiply the number times itself. The cube of a number means you multiply the number times itself three times.

Tips to Remember

- Multiplying Exponential Expressions With the Same Base: Keep the base the same and add the exponents.
- Dividing Exponential Expressions by the Same Base: Subtract the exponents and keep the same base.
- Negative Exponential Expressions: Find the reciprocal.
- Any base raised to the zero power is 1.
- Raising a Power to a Power: Multiply the exponents.

Real Life Applications of Exponents

Exponents are used in scientific notation as shorthand for very large numbers. Instead of writing 6,000,000,000, scientists write 6×10^9. Another use for exponents is in finding the surface area of a room that needs to be painted to determine how much paint is needed. Construction workers use exponents to determine the number of 2 x 4's needed, so they can estimate the costs of construction.

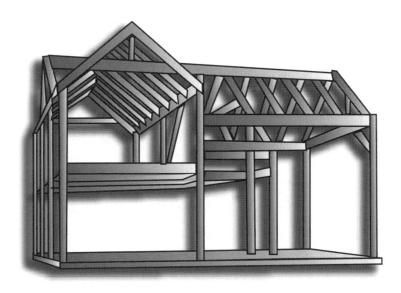

Chapter 6: Square Roots

Introduction to the Concepts of Square Roots

Exponents and roots go together because they turn out to be inverse operations. What one action does, the opposite action undoes. So raising a quantity to the second power is undone by finding the square root. In the previous chapters, inverse operations were introduced. The inverse of addition is subtraction, and the inverse of multiplication is division. This section focuses first on the most common roots used, square roots, and how to interpret, evaluate, and simplify algebraic expressions that include square roots.

Concepts of Square Roots

1 Square Roots and Perfect Squares
2 Rules for Simplifying Radical Expressions

Explanations of Concepts of Square Roots

1 Square Roots and Perfect Squares

A **square root** of a number is found by finding out what number, multiplied by itself, equals that given number. What number, multiplied by itself, equals 25? The answer is 5 because $5 \times 5 = 25$. Using an exponent, you could write $5^2 = 25$. The root number in this example is 5. A radical sign $\sqrt{}$ is used as a symbol to mean "find the square root." The question, "what number multiplied by itself equals 25?" can be written symbolically as $\sqrt{25}$. You can check your answer by multiplying the number times itself.

Some numbers are perfect squares. That means that the square root of that number is a whole number. 100, 25, 16, and 9 are all perfect squares because each has a square root that is a whole number. ($\sqrt{100} = 10$, $\sqrt{25} = 5$, $\sqrt{16} = 4$ and $\sqrt{9} = 3$).

Every number has two square roots—a positive square root and a negative square root. This is because when two negative numbers are multiplied together, their product or answer is a positive number. For example: $-4 \times -4 = 16$ and $4 \times 4 = 16$. So is $\sqrt{16}$ 4 or -4? A radical sign $\sqrt{}$ is used as a symbol to mean "find the principal or **positive** square root." This means that $\sqrt{16} = 4$.

Numbers such as 3 are not perfect squares because the square root is not a whole number. The symbol $\approx$ meaning "is approximately" is used because the number has been rounded off to provide an estimate of the exact root value. The square root of 3 or $\sqrt{3} \approx 1.732$; however, if you multiply 1.732 times 1.732, the answer is 2.999824. If the square root is approximated by rounding to the nearest thousandth, it would be 3.000.

Chapter 6: Square Roots (cont.)

Examples of Square Roots:

Problem: $\sqrt{81}$ =   or the square root of 81 =
What number times itself = 81?

9 x 9 = 81

Answer: Therefore, $\sqrt{81}$ = 9.

Problem: $\sqrt{49}$ = or the square root of 49 =
What number times itself = 49?

7 x 7 = 49

Answer: Therefore, $\sqrt{49}$ = 7.

The above examples were perfect squares. If the number is not a perfect square, then the square root is not a whole number.

Examples of Numbers That Are Not Perfect Squares:

$\sqrt{7} \approx 2.646$
2.646 x 2.646 = 7.001316
Rounded to the nearest hundredth, 7.001316 = 7.00

$\sqrt{11} \approx 3.317$
3.317 x 3.317 = 11.002489
Rounded to the nearest hundredth, 11.002489 = 11.00

Chapter 6: Square Roots (cont.)

2 Rules for Simplifying Radical Expressions

- In simplifying radical expressions, if two numbers are multiplied under the radical sign you may separate the two expressions. First, find the square roots of each one, and then multiply the solutions together.
- If two radical expressions are multiplied together, they can be written as products under the same radical sign.
- You may also find factors for the number under the radical and take the square root of the factors.
- If two numbers are divided under a radical sign, they can be separated into two radicals.
- Multiplying the numerator and denominator of a radical expression by the same number does not change the value.
- Radical expressions can be added and subtracted if each index is the same and each number under the radical sign is the same. The index is the superscript number next to the radical sign that indicates which root to find. $\sqrt[2]{}$ = square root. $\sqrt[3]{}$ = cube root. Most of the time, the ^{2} is left off the radical sign because it is understood that $\sqrt{}$ means "find the square root."
- Radical expressions can be written as fractional exponents. The numerator is the power of the number under the radical sign, and the denominator is the number that is the index.
- Fractional exponents can be changed into radical expressions. The numerator is the exponent of the number under the radical sign, and the denominator is the index.
- Radical expressions are not simplified if there is a radical in the denominator.

Examples of Simplifying Radical Expressions:

If two numbers are multiplied under the radical sign, you may separate the two expressions.

Problem: $\sqrt{(4)(9)} = (\sqrt{4})(\sqrt{9})$

Step 1: Find the square roots of each.

$\sqrt{4} = 2 \qquad \sqrt{9} = 3$

Step 2: Multiply the solutions.

$(2)(3) = 6$

Answer: $\sqrt{(4)(9)} = 6$

Chapter 6: Square Roots (cont.)

If two radical expressions are multiplied together, they can be written as products under the same radical sign.

Problem: $(\sqrt{3})(\sqrt{27}) =$

$\sqrt{(3)(27)} =$

Step 1: Multiply the numbers under the radical. $3 \times 27 = 81$

Step 2: $\sqrt{81}$ the square root of 81 = 9

Answer: $(\sqrt{3})(\sqrt{27}) = 9$

Find factors for the number under the radical, and take the square root of the factors.

Problem: $\sqrt{18}$

Step 1: Find the factors of 18. 2×9 or 3×6

Step 2: 9 is a perfect square, so put the 2×9 under the radical sign.

$\sqrt{(2)(9)}$

Step 3: Remember that parentheses mean multiply the numbers.

$\sqrt{(2)(9)} = (\sqrt{2})(\sqrt{9})$
$\sqrt{9} = 3$
$\sqrt{(2)(9)} = 3\sqrt{2}$

Step 4: The square root of 2 is not a whole number. Rounding it to the nearest thousandth, it is ≈ 1.414
$\sqrt{(2)(9)} \approx 3 \times 1.414$ Note that this is $\approx$ not = because the number has been rounded.

Answer: $\sqrt{(2)(9)} \approx 4.2426$

Chapter 6: Square Roots (cont.)

If two numbers are divided under a radical sign, they can be separated into two radicals.

Problem: $\sqrt{\dfrac{9}{4}}$

Step 1: Put the numbers under two radical signs.

$\dfrac{\sqrt{9}}{\sqrt{4}}$

Step 2: Find the square roots of the numerator and denominator. $\sqrt{9} = 3$ $\sqrt{4} = 2$

Answer: $\sqrt{\dfrac{9}{4}} = \dfrac{3}{2} = 1\dfrac{1}{2}$

Example of Multiplying the numerator and denominator of a radical expression by the same number and not changing the value.

Problem: $\dfrac{5}{\sqrt{3}} =$

Step 1: Construct a fraction with the radical as the numerator and denominator.

$\dfrac{5}{\sqrt{3}} \left(\dfrac{\sqrt{3}}{\sqrt{3}} \right) =$

Remember that a number divided by itself is equal to 1, so the value will not change.

Step 2: Multiply the expression by the fraction. Put the two square roots in the denominator under the same radical.

$\dfrac{5}{\sqrt{3}} \left(\dfrac{\sqrt{3}}{\sqrt{3}} \right) = \dfrac{5\sqrt{3}}{\sqrt{3(3)}} = \dfrac{5\sqrt{3}}{\sqrt{9}}$

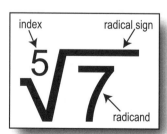

index   radical sign

$\sqrt[5]{7}$

radicand

Step 3: Find the square root of the denominator.

Answer: $\dfrac{5}{\sqrt{3}} = \dfrac{5\sqrt{3}}{\sqrt{9}} = \dfrac{5\sqrt{3}}{3}$

Chapter 6: Square Roots (cont.)

Radical expressions can be added and subtracted if each index is the same and each number under the radical sign is the same.

Examples of Addition and Subtraction of Radical Expressions:

Problem: $3\sqrt{4} + 4\sqrt{4} =$

Step 1: Add the coefficients. $3 + 4 = 7$

Step 2: Bring the radical over. $3\sqrt{4} + 4\sqrt{4} = 7\sqrt{4}$

Problem: $2\sqrt{27} + \sqrt{27} =$

Both have the same index and radicand.

Step 1: Add the coefficients. $2 + 1 = 3$

Step 2: Bring the radical over. $2\sqrt{27} + \sqrt{27} = 3\sqrt{27}$

Problem: $3\sqrt[3]{x} - \sqrt[3]{x} =$

Both have the same index and radicand.

Step 1: Subtract the coefficients. $3 - 1 = 2$

Step 2: Bring the radical over. $3\sqrt[3]{x} - \sqrt[3]{x} = 2\sqrt[3]{x}$

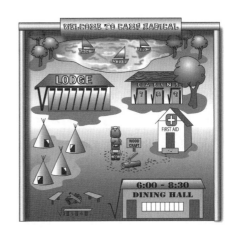

Name: _____ Date: _____

Practice: Square Roots

Directions: Solve and show your work.

Square Roots: Solve and identify which ones are perfect square roots.

1. $\sqrt{4}$ _____

2. $\sqrt{9}$ _____

3. $\sqrt{1}$ _____

4. $\sqrt{25}$ _____

5. $\sqrt{36}$ _____

6. $\sqrt{3}$ _____

7. $\sqrt{2}$ _____

Solve using two radical signs.

8. $\sqrt{(25)(9)}$ _____

9. $\sqrt{(4)(16)}$ _____

10. $\sqrt{16y^2}$ $y > 0$ _____

Solve by multiplying radicals.

11. $(\sqrt{y})(\sqrt{y})$ $y > 0$ _____

12. $(\sqrt{3})(\sqrt{12})$ _____

Name: _____ Date: _____

Chapter 6: Square Roots (cont.)

Solve by factoring.

13. $\sqrt{32}$ _____

14. $\sqrt{125}$ _____

Simplify by dividing radicals.
Remember a radical is not simplified if it has a radical in the denominator.

15. $\sqrt{\dfrac{25}{36}}$ _____

16. $\sqrt{\dfrac{64}{16}}$ _____

17. $\sqrt{\dfrac{4}{3}}$ _____

Solve by adding and subtracting radicals.

18. $3\sqrt{36} + \sqrt{1}$ _____

19. $4\sqrt[5]{x} + 5\sqrt[5]{x}$ _____

20. $6\sqrt[5]{x} + \sqrt[2]{x}$ _____

21. $8\sqrt{5} - 4\sqrt{5}$ _____

22. $9\sqrt{2y} - 3\sqrt{2y}$ _____

Name: _____ Date: _____

Chapter 6: Square Roots (cont.)

Practice: Rooting out the Answers

Exponents and roots are inverse operations.

Directions: Which root is the reciprocal of which square root? Match each item in the second column with the correct reciprocal in the first column.

_____ **1.** 5^2 **A.** 88^2

_____ **2.** 9^2 **B.** 10^2

_____ **3.** $\sqrt{100}$ **C.** $\sqrt{25}$

_____ **4.** $\sqrt{7,744}$ **D.** $\sqrt{81}$

_____ **5.** 55^2 **E.** $\sqrt{484}$

_____ **6.** 6^2 **F.** $\sqrt{2,025}$

_____ **7.** 22^2 **G.** $\sqrt{3,025}$

_____ **8.** $\sqrt{1,296}$ **H.** $\sqrt{36}$

_____ **9.** $\sqrt{400}$ **I.** 36^2

_____ **10.** 45^2 **J.** 20^2

Directions: Simplify the radical expressions.

11. $\sqrt{(16)(9)}$ _____   **12.** $(\sqrt{3})(\sqrt{48})$ _____

13. $\sqrt{\dfrac{16}{4}}$ _____   **14.** $\dfrac{3}{\sqrt{3}}$ _____

15. $4\sqrt{144} + 7\sqrt{144}$ _____

Chapter 6: Square Roots (cont.)

Summary of Roots

A square number is a number that has been multiplied by itself. The exponent tells how many times the number is multiplied by itself. Square roots are found by finding out what number taken times itself equals the number in question. A radical sign $\sqrt{n}$ is used as a symbol for the square root of a number that is represented by the variable n. You can also find cube roots and higher roots. The index is the superscript next to the radical sign that indicates what root to find. Finding the cube root is written as $\sqrt[3]{n}$. The question is "what number multiplied by itself 3 times will equal n?" Higher roots will be represented by $\sqrt[x]{n}$, where x is the variable representing the index of the root and n is the radicand for which you are finding the root.

Tips to Remember

- Square Root: What number times itself equals the number?
- Perfect Squares: The root is a whole number.
- Simplifying Radical Expressions: Use the property rules and rules of operations.

Real Life Applications of Roots

Squares and square roots are used in finding surface area of a square or length of sides. If you know the surface area of the square, that could help find out how much paint is needed for a certain area. Sky divers use radical equations to find the velocity of freefalling using the formula $v = \sqrt{2gd}$.

Chapter 7: Using Algebra to Generalize Patterns

Introduction to Using Algebra to Generalize Patterns

One of the reasons for studying algebra is to see how it can help describe the patterns that are seen in numbers and other applied situations. Patterns are seen everywhere, from the use of bricks in a sidewalk to the way that the leaves form on a tree branch. Most of mathematics revolves around noticing patterns and using them. For example, all of the properties that were reviewed in earlier chapters are the result of patterns. What happens every time you multiply a number by zero? You get zero. That is a pattern that can be observed and generalized into the Zero Multiplication Property. This chapter is a first look at how we can use words and symbols to describe the patterns that we see. The focus will be on trying to move from words to the use of mathematical symbols—the formation of algebraic expressions and equations.

Concepts of Using Algebra to Generalize Patterns

1. Patterns in Number Lists
2. Patterns in Tables

    Input

    Output
3. Algebraic Expressions and Equations
4. Solving Simple Linear Equations

    A. Equal Additions Rule

    B. Equal Multiplications Rule

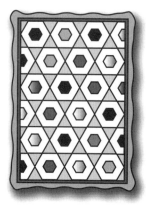

Explanations of Concepts of Using Algebra to Generalize Patterns

1   Patterns in Number Lists

One of the places to look for patterns is in lists of number. Once we see a pattern, we can describe it in words or describe it using variables and numbers. Describing the pattern is a way of communicating the rule being used to form the list of numbers. Let's consider some examples.

Example: 2, 4, 6, 8, … is the beginning of an infinite list of numbers.
- What number would come next in the list?   10
- Why? What pattern do you see? What is the rule?

Chapter 7: Using Algebra to Generalize Patterns (cont.)

In Words: The list is a list of even numbers starting at 2. To get the next entry, just add two to the previous number in the list.

In Symbols: The first entry = 2 = 1 • 2

The second entry = 4 = 2 • 2

The third entry = 6 = 3 • 2

Notice the pattern of entry position times 2 to get the number in the list. So, the nth number in the list will be $n • 2$.

Example: 1, 5, 9, 13, … is the beginning of an infinite list of numbers.

- What number would come next in the list? 17
- Why? What pattern do you see? What is the rule?

In Words: To get the next entry, just add 4 to the previous number in the list.

In Symbols: The first entry = 1

The second entry = 5 = 1 + 4 (previous entry plus 4) = 1 + 1 • 4

The third entry = 9 = 5 + 4 = (1 + 4) + 4 = 1 + (4 + 4) = 1 + 2 • 4

The fourth entry = 13 = 9 + 4 = 1 + 4 + 4 + 4 = 1 + 3 • 4

Do you notice the pattern? How would you find the tenth entry in the list?

The tenth entry = 1 + 9 • 4 = 37 because you add 1 and 1 less than the entry times 4.

❷ Patterns in Tables

Patterns can be revealed in tables of information from which a general rule can be described. A table typically shows an input value or number and the related output value or number. By looking at the information given in the table, the rule used to transform the input number into the output number can be discovered. Again, this rule can be described in words or by using mathematical symbols. Let's consider some examples and see if we can answer the question, "What's the rule?"

Example:

Input	Output
3	2
-1	-2
11	10
0	-1

Chapter 7: Using Algebra to Generalize Patterns (cont.)

- Based on the pattern you see in the table, if 7 is the input, what is the output?
  6
- Why? What pattern do you see? What is the rule?

In words: Take the input number and subtract 1 from it to get the output.

In symbols: If n is the input number, then $n - 1$ is the output number.

Example:

Input	Output
3	8
0	2
-4	-6
5	12

- Based on the pattern you see in the table, if 7 is the input, what is the output?   16
- Why? What pattern do you see? What is the rule?

In words: Take the input number, double it, and add 2 to get the output number.

In symbols: If n is the input number, then $2n + 2$ is the output number.

③ Algebraic Expressions and Equations

Being able to describe rules using symbols means we are forming and working with algebraic expressions and equations. In earlier work, the word *term* was defined to mean a number, variable, or product of numbers and variables. An algebraic expression is a combination of numbers, variables, and operations. In other words, it consists of terms that are combined using addition, subtraction, multiplication, or division. For example, $2x^2 + 3y$ is an example of an algebraic expression. To have an equation, an equal sign is used to show how two algebraic expressions are related. For example, $2x^2 + 3y = 5x(6 + y^4)$ is an equation. Many times, the start of work in algebra requires that information (from number lists, tables, or other sources) be put into algebraic form—an expression or equation that describes that situation. Practice is needed to translate from words into symbols.

Chapter 7: Using Algebra to Generalize Patterns (cont.)

Examples:

Translate into symbols: The number of chairs needed is twice the number of tables.

We can use symbols (c for chairs and t for tables) and translate the situation into an equation, $c = 2t$.

Translate into symbols: Fifteen more than three times a number.

Let x be the number. Then three times the number becomes $3x$ and to get 15 more, means addition. Final form: $3x + 15$.

④ Solving Simple Linear Equations

One of the first actions in working with equations is the ability to solve an equation. To solve an equation means to find number values that make the equation true. Depending on the type of equation, you may find no solution, one solution, two solutions, and so on. To begin work in solving equations, let's focus on just one type—the simplest type—and see how to use what we know about number properties to find the solution. The simplest type of equation is called a linear equation. A **linear equation** can have number terms and variable terms—but the variable is raised only to the first power—so no squares or roots or any other exponents can be present.

Examples of Linear Equations:

$$7 = 2x + 4$$
$$3x + 3 = \text{-}11$$
$$6y + 7 = 9y - 4$$

Not Examples of Linear Equations:

$$7x^2 + 5 = 6$$
$$12 + \sqrt{x} = 16$$

Linear equations will have only one solution. And solving linear equations is simply a matter of keeping the balance in the equation — and using what you know about inverses. Remember that addition and subtraction are inverse operations and multiplication and division are inverse operations. Consider some simple examples solving linear equations.

Chapter 7: Using Algebra to Generalize Patterns (cont.)

Ⓐ   Equal Additions Rule

To undo addition, subtract the same amount from both sides. To undo subtraction, add the same amount to both sides. The new equation is equivalent to the original.

Example: $x + 6 = 15$

Now, we know without algebra what the solution to this equation would be—just answer the question 6 plus what is 15? But let's use what we know about inverses and balance to find the solution algebraically.

We want to "solve for x," meaning we want to exchange the given equation for one that looks like, $x =$ the answer. Basically, this means we want to isolate x by itself on one side of the equation.

Step 1: Look at the equation, $x + 6 = 15$. What is in the way? The 6. If we move it, the x is alone and we have a solution! How do we move it? In the original equation, the 6 is added, so the inverse is to subtract. To keep the balance in an equation—the equality—we will need to subtract 6 from the right side of the equation, too. So,

$$x + 6 = 15$$

Step 2: $x + 6 - 6 = 15 - 6$

$$x = 9 \ \text{(since } 6 - 6 = 0 \text{ and } 15 - 6 = 9)$$

Check: This means the original equation is true when we substitute 9 for x and compute,

$$9 + 6 = 15$$

Ⓑ   Equal Multiplications Rule

To undo multiplication, divide by the same amount on both sides of the equation. To undo division, multiply by the same amount on both sides. The new equation is equivalent to the original equation.

Example: $3 \cdot x = 33$

Now, we know without algebra what the solution to this equation would be—just answer the question "3 times what is 33?" But let's use what we know about inverses and balance to find the solution algebraically.

Chapter 7: Using Algebra to Generalize Patterns (cont.)

We want to "solve for x," meaning we want to exchange the given equation for one that looks like, $x =$ the answer. Basically, this means we want to isolate x by itself on one side of the equation.

Step 1: Look at the equation, $3 \cdot x = 33$. What is in the way? The 3. If we move it, the x is alone and we have a solution! How do we move it? The 3 is multiplied by the x, so the inverse operation is to divide. In an equation, to keep the balance—the equality—we will need to divide by 3 on the right side of the equation, too. So,

Step 2:
$$3 \cdot x = 33$$
$$\frac{3 \cdot x}{3} = \frac{33}{3}$$
$$x = 11 \text{ (since } \tfrac{3}{3} = 1 \text{ and } \tfrac{33}{3} = 11)$$

Check: This means the original equation is true when we substitute 11 for x and compute,

$$3 \cdot 11 = 33$$

Example: Find the solution for $5 + 2x = 25$

Step 1: To isolate x, start by removing the 5. Subtract 5 from both sides.

$$5 + 2x = 25$$
$$\underline{-5 \qquad\quad -5}$$
$$2x = 20$$

$$\frac{2x}{2} = \frac{20}{2}$$

Step 2: Now, to undo multiplication by 2, divide both sides by 2.

$$x = 10$$

The solution is 10.

Check: Replace x with 10 in the original equation and check.
$$5 + 2(10) = 25$$

Chapter 7: Using Algebra to Generalize Patterns (cont.)

Practice: Moving From Words to Symbols

Directions: Complete the following exercises.

1. Fill in the next numbers in the list:

   A) 1, 1, 2, 3, 5, 8, _____, _____, _____, …

   B) Describe, in words, how you find the next numbers in the list. _____

   _____

   _____

   _____

2. Fill in the next numbers in the sequence:

   A) 1, 3, 6, 10, _____, _____, _____, …

   B) What would the tenth number in the list be? _____

   C) Describe, in words, how you find the next numbers in the pattern. _____

   _____

   _____

   _____

3. For the input/output table, find each of the following:

Input	Output
2	-3
0	-5
-4	-9
5	0

   A) If the input is 21, what will the output be? _____

   B) Describe the rule in words: _____

   _____

   C) Describe the rule in symbols: If n is the input, _____

   _____

4. For the input/output table, find each of the following:

Input	Output
1	2
3	12
-2	2
-4	12
0	0

   A) If the input is -5, what will the output be? _____

   B) Describe the rule in words: _____

   _____

   C) Describe the rule in symbols: If n is the input, _____

   _____

Name: _____ Date: _____

Chapter 7: Using Algebra to Generalize Patterns (cont.)

Translate each into an algebraic expression or equation. Label each answer as EXP (expression) or EQ (equation).

5. Seven times the square of a number. _____

6. Five more than twice the number. _____

7. The sum of the number and the number increased by one is fifteen. _____

8. Twelve less than the number of people invited. _____

9. The difference in two numbers is one-half the sum of the two numbers. _____

Solve each linear equation.

10. $-3x = 21$ _____

11. $m + 5 = 12$ _____

12. $7 = 5 + 2x$ _____

13. $3x + 10 = -26$ _____

14. $3b + 7 + 2b = 13$ _____

15. $x + 2 = -20$ _____

Name: _____ Date: _____

Chapter 7: Using Algebra to Generalize Patterns (cont.)

Practice: More Moving From Words to Symbols

Directions: Complete the following exercises.

1. Fill in the next numbers in the list:

    A)   1, 3, 4, 7, 11, 18, _____, _____, _____, …

    B)   Describe, in words, how you find the next numbers in the list. _____

    _____

    _____

    _____

2. Fill in the next numbers in the sequence:

    A)   1, 2, 4, 8, 16, 32, _____, _____, …

    B)   What would the tenth number in the list be? _____

    C)   Describe, in words, how you find the next numbers in the pattern. _____

    _____

    _____

    _____

3. For the input/output table, find each of the following:

Input	Output
2	9
0	7
-9	-2
-20	-8

    A)   If the input is 30, what will the output be? _____

    B)   Describe the rule in words: _____

    _____

    C)   Describe the rule in symbols: If n is the input, _____

    _____

4. For the input/output table, find each of the following:

Input	Output
1	-6
3	-4
-2	-9
-4	-11
0	-7

    A)   If the input is 5, what will the output be? _____

    B)   Describe the rule in words: _____

    _____

    C)   Describe the rule in symbols: If n is the input, _____

    _____

Name: _____ Date: _____

Chapter 7: Using Algebra to Generalize Patterns (cont.)

Translate each into an algebraic expression or equation. Label each answer as EXP (expression) or EQ (equation).

5. five times the cube of a number. _____

6. Five more than four times the number. _____

7. The sum of the number and the number decreased by one is fifteen. _____

8. Twelve more than the number of apples in the basket. _____

9. The difference in two numbers is one-fourth the sum of the two numbers.

_____

Solve each linear equation.

10. $-5x = 35$ _____

11. $a + 5 = 37$ _____

12. $23 = 1 + 2x$ _____

13. $4x + 10 = -26$ _____

14. $5b + 7 + 2b = 23$ _____

15. $2x + 4 = -16$ _____

Chapter 7: Using Algebra to Generalize Patterns (cont.)

Summary of Using Algebra to Generalize Patterns

Words and symbols can be used to describe patterns. Patterns can be found in lists of numbers and in data tables. Mathematical symbols can also be used to describe patterns through the formation of algebraic expressions and equations. Algebraic expressions are combinations of numbers, variables, and the operations of addition, subtraction, multiplication, and division. Algebraic equations use an equal sign to show how two algebraic expresssions are related.

- **Equal Addition Rule:** To undo addition, subtract the same amount from both sides. To undo subtraction, add the same amount to both sides. The new equation is equivalent to the original.

- **Equal Multiplication Rule:** To undo multiplication, divide by the same amount on both sides of the equation. To undo division, multiply by the same amount on both sides. The new equation is equivalent to the original equation.

Tips to Remember

When you're solving equations, think of each side sitting on a balance scale. Every action completed on one side must be balanced by the equivalent action on the other side. Keeping the balance means treating each side of the equation equally.

Real Life Applications of Using Algebra to Generalize Patterns

Patterns are observed everywhere in the real world. In manufacturing, patterns for production, costs, and quantities of material to be used are all important for setting up the models for predicting sales and profits. Patterns are even observable in nature—did you know there is a pattern connecting the number of times a cricket chirps and temperature? Algebra allows us to generalize—make rules—that describe everyday life situations and solve problems that arise from these situations.

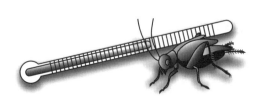

Chapter 8: Problem-Solving Strategies

Introduction to Problem Solving

One of the major goals of algebra is to solve problems. In solving problems there are many strategies that can be used. Some strategies include Making a Table and Guess, Check, and Revise to solve linear problems. Algebra uses equations to solve linear problems using variables. An equation uses numbers and variables to describe the relationship between two or more quantities. An equation is a mathematical statement with an = sign in it. Variables are letters used to identify an unknown number. There are many kinds of equations, but the most commonly used in algebra are linear equations. This section covers strategies for problem solving and using linear equations to solve problems.

Concepts

1 Problem Solving

2 Problem-Solving Strategies

   A Making Tables

   B Guess, Check, and Revise

   C Using Linear Equations to Solve Problems

Explanations of Problem-Solving Concepts

1 Problem Solving

When trying to solve a problem, it helps to have a systematic plan. One way of solving problems is using models. George Polya was a mathematician who devised a four-step plan for problem solving.

1. Understand the Problem
   - Identify what is known
   - What are you asked to find?
   - Can you state the question in your own words?

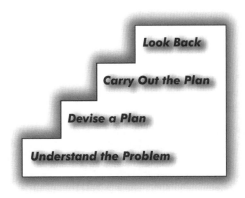

Chapter 8: Problem-Solving Strategies (cont.)

2. Devise a Plan—Choose a Strategy
    - Would a table help organize the information?
    - Would a diagram or picture help?
    - Can I make a first estimate, test, and revise to find the solution? (Guess, Check, and Revise)
    - Can I use a variable or write an equation that can be solved?

3. Carry Out the Plan—Put the Strategy to Work
    - Construct and fill in the table.
    - Draw the picture or diagram.
    - Make your best guess and follow through with tests and revision (Guess, Check and Revise).
    - Solve the equation.

4. Look back
    - You have a solution.
    - Does it make sense? Is it reasonable?
    - Did you check your work?
    - Is there another approach that would give you the same answer?

Example Problem Solving Using Polya's Process:

The costs for speeding tickets are determined in some states by fining the person a flat rate of $25 plus $20 for every mile per hour over the speed limit. The speed limit was 55. If a person was fined $225, how fast was he or she going?

1. Understand the Problem
    Identify what is known

    Flat rate is $25.

    Fine is $20 per mph over the limit.

    Total fine was $225.

    Speed limit was 55.

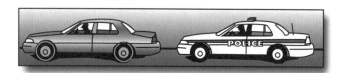

Chapter 8: Problem-Solving Strategies (cont.)

What do we want to know? How fast was the driver going?

How many miles over the limit was the driver driving?

2.   Devise a Plan, and

3.   Carry Out the Plan

For this problem, any one of three strategies could work. Each strategy will be shown showing the final answer is the same in all three cases.

② Problem-Solving Strategies

Ⓐ   Make a Table Strategy

# of Miles over the Limit	1	2	3	4	5	6	7	8	9	10
Cost of Fine	25 + 20(1) = 45	25 + 20(2)= 65	85	105	125	145	165	185	205	225

In filling out the table, the fine costs rise by $20 for each mph. Following the pattern, the fine of $225 is reached when the input of 10 miles over the speed limit is used.

Note your table could have had entries by 2s or considered inputs by 5s. Different choices would mean fewer or more trials to find the answer needed.

The solution of 10 mph over the limit checks out for a fine of $225. Have we answered the question?

Ⓐ   Guess, Check, and Revise

Guess: Speed of the car was 75 mph.

That would mean that 75 − 55 = 20, and car was 20 mph over the limit.

Fine would be: fine = $25 + $20 (20) = $425

Revise: $425 is too high, so we need to guess a car speed lower than 75.

Chapter 8: Problem-Solving Strategies (cont.)

Guess: Speed of the car was 65.

That would mean, since 65 − 55 = 10, the car was traveling 10 mph over the limit.

Fine would be: fine = $25 + $20(10) = $225

That matches the given information! The car was traveling 10 mph over the speed limit of 55 mph.

The solution checks out. Have we answered the question?

Ⓒ Using Linear Equations to Solve Problems

Write the equation to describe the relationship between miles over the limit and cost of ticket.

Let x represent the number of miles over the 55 mph speed limit of the car.
Then, flat rate of $25 plus $20 per mile over limit should equal the total fine, $225. Translate that into an equation,

$$25 + 20x = 225$$

Solve the equation.
- We want to find the value of x that makes the equation work. We want to isolate x by itself, or sometimes we say, "solve for x."
- Consider the equation. What is the first thing in the way of getting x by itself? The 25. How do we undo addition? Subtract! Just be sure to keep the balance by subtracting the same amount from each side of the equation.

$$\begin{array}{r} 25 + 20x = 225 \\ -25 \qquad\quad -25 \\ \hline 20x = 200 \end{array}$$

Chapter 8: Problem-Solving Strategies (cont.)

- What do you need to do next to find out what the value of x is? The only thing left is the 20 being multiplied by x. How do you undo multiplication? Divide! Just be sure to keep the balance of the equation by dividing both sides by the same amount.

$$20x = 200$$

$$\frac{20x}{20} = \frac{200}{20}$$

$$x = 10$$

- Check your work using the answer. If you are 10 mph over the speed limit, your fine is,

$$\$25 + \$20(10) = \$25 + \$200 = \$225$$

4. Look Back

Using each of the strategies, it was determined that the driver was 10 mph over the speed limit.

Have we answered the question asked in the original problem?

No, we need to know the speed of the car when ticketed. The driver went 10 miles over the 55 mph speed limit. The driver was going $10 + 55 = 65$ miles per hour.

Name: _____ Date: _____

Chapter 8: Problem-Solving Strategies (cont.)

Practice: Problem Solving

Directions: Show your work to solve these problems.

Problem Solving

1. Dan has $10 more than Chris. Together they have $80. How much money does each one have?

   _____

2. The concession stand sold twice as much cola as it did orange soda and three times as much bottled water as orange soda. A total of 600 drinks were sold. How many bottles of water were sold?

   _____

3. Most bacteria divide every 20 minutes. Starting with one bacteria, how many bacteria will be present in three hours?

   _____

Using Linear Equations to Solve Problems

4. $x + 4 = 0$ _____

5. $5b + 3 = 28$ _____

6. $2x - 12 = 8$ _____

7. $5y - 1 = 124$ _____

Name: _____ Date: _____

Chapter 8: Problem-Solving Strategies (cont.)

Write an equation to solve the following problems.

8. A board is 12 feet long. It is sawed into two pieces. One piece is 0.5 feet longer than the other. How many feet long is each piece?

   _____

9. Tyrone has four times as many books as Lei. Together they have 50 books. How many books does each have?

   _____

10. There are 12 people on a jury. Four more jurors voted to convict than voted not to convict the person on trial. How many voted to convict?

   _____

11. Laticia had 8 fewer pencils than Kim. They had a total of 20 pencils. How many did each have?

   _____

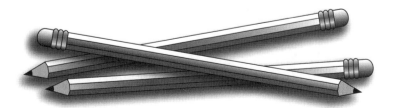

Name: _____   Date: _____

Chapter 8: Problem-Solving Strategies (cont.)

Practice: What Is the Problem?

1. Your house has a concrete foundation that is 20 cm above the ground. You add six layers of cement blocks to the foundation. Each layer adds 8 cm to the height of the pile.

    A. Find the pattern and complete the table.

# of Layers	0	1	2	3	4	5	6	7	8	9
Height in cm	20	28	36	44	52	60	68			

    B. Draw a graph of the relationship between the number of layers and the height of the wall.

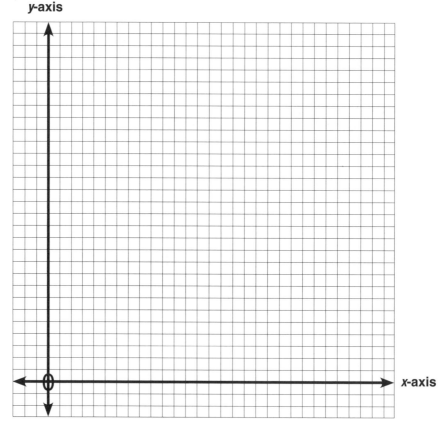

    C. Using the graph, determine how high the wall would be if you had 12 layers.

    _____

    D. Write an equation to represent this relationship. _____

Name: _____ Date: _____

Chapter 8: Problem-Solving Strategies (cont.)

2. A high school has a single-elimination basketball tournament with eight teams. They need to pay the referees $50 each per game. There are two referees in each game.

   A. Use the diagram to determine how much money the school needs to pay the referees for the tournament.

   _____

   B. Write an equation to show how much the school should pay the referees.

   _____

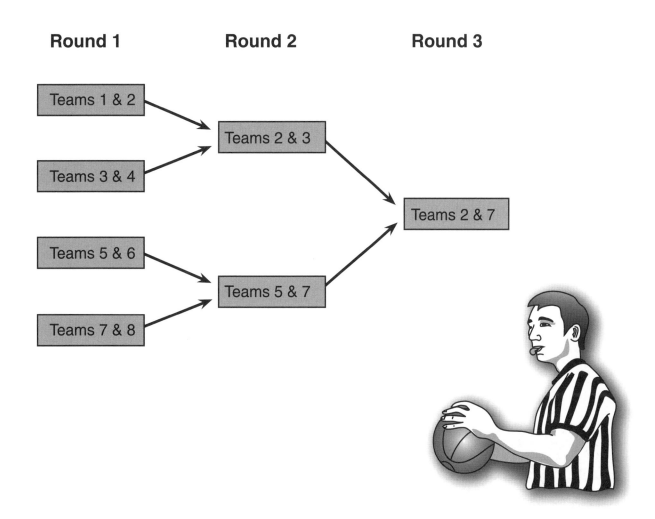

Round 1   **Round 2**   **Round 3**

Teams 1 & 2

Teams 3 & 4

Teams 2 & 3

Teams 5 & 6

Teams 7 & 8

Teams 5 & 7

Teams 2 & 7

Name: _____ Date: _____

Chapter 8: Problem-Solving Strategies (cont.)

3. You have a fish aquarium that is 30 cm off the floor. The aquarium is 100 cm high. You fill the aquarium with water at the rate of 8 cm per minute.

   A. How many cm above the floor will the water level be after 15 minutes? Use a linear equation and graph to solve the problem.

   _____

   B. Create a graph to show the relationship between the height of the water above the floor and the time the water is flowing in.

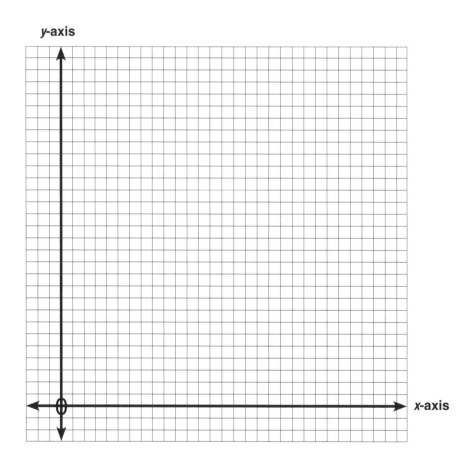

y-axis

x-axis

Chapter 8: Problem-Solving Strategies (cont.)

Summary of Problem-Solving Strategies

Problems can be solved in a variety of ways. This section introduced you to Polya's four stages of problem solving:

- Understand the Problem
- Devise a Plan—Choose a Strategy!
- Carry Out the Plan—Put the Strategy to Work
- Look Back

You were introduced to verbal models, making tables, graphs, looking for patterns, using models, and diagrams. One strategy is using a verbal and algebraic model to solve problems.

To solve a problem:
- Identify the information that you already know.
- Use a variable to identify the information that you do not know.
- Write the problem as an equation.
- Solve the equation.

In solving equations:
- Simplify each side of the equation using the rules for the order of operations.
- What do you need to do to find out what the variable is? There are two possible steps:
  1. Add and/or subtract the same number and or variable from both sides of the equation.
  2. Multiply and/or divide both sides of the equation by the same number.
- Always look back! Check your work using the answer.

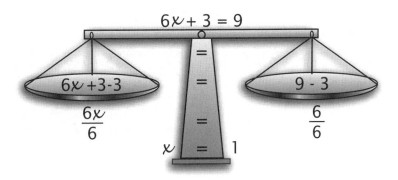

Chapter 8: Problem-Solving Strategies (cont.)

Tips to Remember

Scientists have discovered that using "THE" scientific method to solve problems leads to the misconception that there is only one way to solve problems. The authors do not want to leave you with the misconception that there is only one "right" way to solve problems. The Polya Process, looking for patterns, using models and diagrams, making tables, and using equations are only a few strategies for solving problems. There are many problem-solving strategies. Students sometimes use different methods to get the same answers. Students need to use what makes sense to them when solving problems.

Real Life Applications of Using Linear Equations to Solve Problems

Linear equations can be used in studying the speed of different wildlife, population studies, page layout and design, temperature change, marine biology, framing pictures, and finding costs, rates, averages, and percentages. Linear equations are also used in ecology, chemistry, retail sales, and purchasing.

Answer Keys

Chapter 1: Basic Concepts of Numbers
Practice: Which Number Is Which? (page 13)

Number	Type or Types
1. 8	Real, Rational, Natural, Whole, Integer
2. 0	Real, Rational, Whole, Integer
3. -6	Real, Rational, Integer
4. $\frac{1}{4}$	Real, Rational
5. -450	Real, Rational, Integer
6. $\sqrt{9}$	Real, Rational, Natural, Integer, Whole
7. $-\frac{21}{23}$	Real, Rational
8. 0.12122122212222…	Real, Irrational
9. $0.\overline{0367}$	Real, Rational
10. $\sqrt{11}$	Real, Irrational

Chapter 1: Basic Concepts of Numbers
Practice: Numbers—Are They Real? (page 14)

Chapter 2: Operations of Numbers and Variables
Practice: Addition and Subtraction of Numbers and Variables (page 19)

1. $335 + 1{,}567 = 1{,}902$

2. $3a + 12a + 1a = 16a$

3. $3a + 24b + 4c =$ Unlike terms cannot be added.

4. $8x + 9x = 17x$

Answer Keys (cont.)

5. $\frac{1}{2}x + 5x = 5\frac{1}{2}x$

6. $5a + a = 6a$

7. $18 + 9 = 27$

8. $8 + c =$ Unlike terms cannot be added.

9. $4x - 8y =$ Unlike terms cannot be subtracted.

10. $35 - 10 = 25$

11. $7 - \frac{1}{2} = 6\frac{1}{2}$

12. $123a - 5a = 118a$

13. $2,345 - 5z =$ Unlike terms cannot be subtracted.

14. $435a - 37a = 398a$

Chapter 2: Operations of Numbers and Variables
Practice: Multiplication of Numbers and Variables (page 22)

1. $7y \cdot 8z = 56yz$

2. $27 \cdot 56 = 1,512$

3. $10a \cdot 35a = 350a^2$

4. $a \cdot b = ab$

5. $22 \cdot 4a = 88a$

6. $b \cdot b = b^2$

7. $5y \cdot 9 = 45y$

8. $25 \cdot 33y = 825y$

9. $21 \cdot b = 21b$

10. $38 \cdot 9 = 342$

Chapter 2: Operations of Numbers and Variables
Practice: Division of Numbers and Variables (page 25)

1. $\frac{3}{8} \div \frac{1}{8} = 3$

2. $800 \div 50 = 16$

3. $36.9 \div 2.4 = 15.375$

4. $2.5 \overline{)37.5} = 15$

5. $\frac{300}{25} = 12$

6. $225x \div 3x = 75$

Answer Keys (cont.)

7. $35x \div 7xy = 5y$

8. $\dfrac{3x}{4x} = 0.75$

9. $\dfrac{8x}{2y} = 4\dfrac{x}{y}$

10. $\dfrac{8ab}{b} = 8a$

Chapter 2: Operations of Numbers and Variables
Practice: Addition, Subtraction, Multiplication, and Division by Zero (page 27)

1. $5 + 0 = 5$
2. $0 + \frac{1}{4} = \frac{1}{4}$
3. $0 + y = y$
4. $7 - 0 = 7$
5. $0 - 13 = -13$
6. $0 - (-12) = 12$
7. $0 - b = -b$
8. $55 - 0 = 55$
9. $a \bullet 0 = 0$
10. $2{,}000 \bullet 0 = 0$
11. $8xyz \bullet 0 = 0$
12. $0 \bullet 9 = 0$
13. $0 \bullet y = 0$
14. $0 \bullet \frac{1}{4} = 0$
15. $0 \div 4 = 0$
16. $0 \div f = 0$
17. $3 \div 0 =$ You cannot divide a number by 0.
18. $ab \div 0 =$ You cannot divide a number by 0.

Answer Keys (cont.)

Chapter 2: Operations of Numbers and Variables
Practice: Order of Operations (page 30)

1. $(20 - 2) \div 3 =$ $18 \div 3 = 6$

2. $26 + (4 \div 2) =$ $26 + 2 = 28$

3. $3(3 + 5) =$ $3(8) = 24$

4. $2(6 - 3) - 3 =$ $2(3) - 3 = 6 - 3 = 3$

5. $2 \times 9^2 =$ $2 \times 81 = 162$

6. $6 - 3^2 \div 2 =$ $6 - 9 \div 2 = 6 - \frac{9}{2} = 6 - 4.5 = 1.5$

7. $3 \times 5 + 4 \times 10 =$ $15 + 40 = 55$

8. $30 \div 5 - 24 \div 6 =$ $6 - 4 = 2$

9. $25 \div 5 + 24 \div 6 =$ $5 + 4 = 9$

10. $3 \times 6 + 4 \times 35 =$ $18 + 140 = 158$

11. $6 \times 5 - 4 \times 5 =$ $30 - 20 = 10$

12. $9 \div 3 - 10 \div 5 =$ $3 - 2 = 1$

13. $3(6 - 3) + 6 \times 2 =$ $3(3) + 12 = 9 + 12 = 21$

14. $(6 - 1)^2 - 5 \times 2 =$ $(5)^2 - 10 = 25 - 10 = 15$

15. $6 \div (1 + 2) - 2 =$ $\frac{6}{3} - 2 = 2 - 2 = 0$

16. $10 + 3^2 - 2 + 3 =$ $10 + 9 - 2 + 3 = 19 - 2 + 3 = 17 + 3 = 20$

17. $22 - 2 \times 5 + 4 =$ $22 - 10 + 4 = 12 + 4 = 16$

18. $2 - 7(7) + 50 =$ $2 - 49 + 50 = -47 + 50 = 3$

19. $5(6 - 2) - 3 =$ $5(4) - 3 = 20 - 3 = 17$

20. $(5 + 6) \times 8 =$ $11 \times 8 = 88$

Chapter 2: Operations of Numbers and Variables (page 31)
Practice: Smooth Operator

1. C   2. B   3. D   4. A

5. B, G   6. C   7. A, E, F   8. D   9. B   10. A   11. E

12. parentheses, multiplication, addition

13. parentheses, exponents, multiplication, subtraction

14. parentheses, division, subtraction

15. parentheses, exponents, multiplication, addition

Answer Keys (cont.)

Chapter 3: Working With Integers and Signed Numbers
Practice: Working With Integers and Signed Numbers—It's all just ADDITION! (page 41)

1. $5 - -3 = 5 + 3 = 8$
2. $-17 + -9 = -26$
3. $|0| = 0$
4. $-24 + 56 = 32$
5. $|-21| = 21$
6. $15 - -8 = 23$
7. $|73| = 73$
8. $45 + -19 = 26$
9. $|-7 + -3| = |-10| = 10$
10. $|2 - -13| = |2 + 13| = |15| = 15$

Chapter 3: Working With Integers and Signed Numbers
Practice: Coasting Between Multiplication and Division (page 44)

1. $-7 \times 3 = -21$
2. $20 \times -5 = -100$
3. $0 \div 7 = 0$
4. $100 \div -10 = -10$
5. $11 \times -3 = -33$
6. $-36 \div 6 = -6$
7. $-2 \times -8 = 16$
8. $-72 \div -6 = 12$
9. $-3(6 + -2) = -3(4) = -12$
10. $12 \div -6 + 4 - -7 = (12 \div -6) + 4 - -7 = -2 + 4 - -7 = 2 - -7 = 2 + 7 = 9$

Chapter 3: Working With Integers and Signed Numbers
Practice: All Numbers, All Signs, Let's Operate! (page 46)

1. $-\frac{3}{5} \times \frac{7}{8} = -\frac{21}{40}$
2. $7.8 + -5.3 = 2.5$
3. $-110 \div 2.5 = -44$
4. $5\sqrt{3} + -11\sqrt{3} = -6\sqrt{3}$

Answer Keys (cont.)

5. $-2.3 \times -10.2 = 23.46$

6. $5 \times -36 = -180$

7. $-\frac{2}{3} + \frac{5}{6} = -\frac{4}{6} + \frac{5}{6} = \frac{1}{6}$

8. $-\frac{10}{11} \div \frac{15}{22} = -\frac{10}{11} \times \frac{22}{15} = -\frac{4}{3} = -1\frac{1}{3}$

9. $2(4.7 + -3.6) = 2.2$

10. $|-7 - -3.5| = 3.5$

Chapter 3: Working With Integers and Signed Numbers
Practice: Integers and Signed Numbers (page 47)

1. $-33 + -9 = -42$

2. $-24 + 56 = 32$

3. $|-33| = 33$

4. $15 - -8 = 23$

5. $|88| = 88$

6. $|-8 + -35| = |-43| = 43$

7. $|2 - -13| = |2 + 13| = |15| = 15$

8. $-5 \times 15 = -75$

9. $-3 \times -9 = 27$

10. $-432 \div -6 = 72$

11. $-3(8 + -3) = -3(5) = -15$

12. $24 \div -6 + 4 - -7 = (24 \div -6) + 4 - -7 = -4 + 4 - -7 = 0 + 7 = 7$

13. $-\frac{3}{7} \times \frac{7}{8} = -\frac{21}{56} = -\frac{3}{8}$

14. $6\sqrt{5} + -11\sqrt{5} = -5\sqrt{5}$

15. $-\frac{10}{13} \div \frac{16}{26} = -\frac{10}{13} \times \frac{26}{16} = -\frac{5}{1} \times \frac{2}{8} = -\frac{10}{8} = -\frac{5}{4} = -1\frac{1}{4}$

16. $|-9 - -3.5| = |-9 + 3.5| = |-5.5| = 5.5$

Chapter 4: Properties of Numbers
Practice: Properties of Numbers (pages 56–57)

		Simplify	Property
1.	$6 + 0 =$	6	Identity Property of Addition
2.	$0 + c =$	c	Identity Property of Addition
3.	$2b + 0 =$	$2b$	Identity Property of Addition

Answer Keys (cont.)

4. $8 \times 1 =$ 8   Identity Property of Multiplication

5. $1 \times 350 =$ 350   Identity Property of Multiplication

6. $b \cdot 1 =$ b Identity Property of Multiplication

7. $3 + 7 = 7 + 3$ $10 = 10$ Commutative Property of Addition

8. $\frac{1}{5} \times 1 =$ $\frac{1}{5}$ Identity Property of Multiplication

9. $\frac{1}{5} \times 0 = 0 \times \frac{1}{5}$ $0 = 0$ Commutative Property of Multiplication

10. $3y \cdot 7 = 7 \cdot 3y$ $21y = 21y$ Commutative Property of Multiplication

11. $a + b = b + a$ $a + b = b + a$ Commutative Property of Addition

12. $7 \times 9 = 9 \times 7$ $63 = 63$ Commutative Property of Multiplication

13. $(3 + 9) + 7 = 3 + (9 + 7)$ $19 = 19$ Associative Property of Addition

14. $\frac{5x}{5} =$ x Inverse Operations

15. $(3 \times 4) \times 8 = 3 \times (4 \times 8)$ $96 = 96$ Associative Property of Multiplication

16. $(d \cdot b) \cdot c = d \cdot (b \cdot c)$ $dbc = dbc$ Associative Property of Multiplication

17. $x - 7 + 7 =$ x Inverse Operations

18. $5 - 6 + 6 =$ 5   Inverse Operations

19. $3(5 + 2) = 3 \times 5 + 3 \times 2$ 21   Distributive Property of Multiplication Over Addition

20. $a(b + c) = a \cdot b + a \cdot c$ $a(b + c) = ab + ac$ Distributive Property of Multiplication Over Addition

21. $a \cdot \frac{1}{a} =$ 1   Reciprocal or Multiplicative Inverse Operations

Chapter 4: Properties of Numbers
Practice: Whose Property Is It? (page 58)

1. E   2. D   3. F   4. B   5. I   6. C   7. H   8. G   9. A

10. zero

11. It identifies the original number.

12. one

13. It identifies the original number.

14. Inverse operations are operations that cancel each other or undo the other operation.

Answer Keys (cont.)

Chapter 5: Exponents and Exponential Expressions
Practice: Exponents and Exponential Expressions (pages 69–70)

1. $10^2 =$ 100

2. $5^5 =$ 3,125

3. $6^{10} =$ 60,466,176

4. $100^0 =$ 1 Any number raised to the ^{0} power is 1.

5. $y^0 =$ 1 Any variable raised to the ^{0} power is 1.

6. $3(5)^2 =$ $3(25) = 75$

7. $5(-3)^3 =$ $5(-27) = -135$

8. $10(b)^2 =$ $10(b^2) = 10b^2$

9. $10(z^3) + 2(z^3)$ $10 + 2 = 12$ $= 12(z^3) = 12z^3$

10. $2(4^3) + (4^3)$ $2 + 1$ $= 3(4^3) = 3(64) = 192$

11. $5(z^3) - 3(z^3)$ $5 - 3 = 2$ $= 2(z^3) = 2z^3$

12. $7(2^3) - 3(2^3)$ $7 - 3 = 4$ $= 4(2^3) = 4(8) = 32$

13. $3(z^3) - 1(z)$ Exponents are not the same and cannot be subtracted.

14. $(z^3)(z^4)$ $^{3+4=7}$ $= z^7$

15. $(a^3)(a^2)$ $^{3+2=5}$ $= a^5$

16. $3^2 \div 3$ Both roots are 3. $^{2-1=1}$ $= 3^1 = 3$

17. $x^4 \div x^2$ Both roots are x. $^{4-2=2}$ $= x^2$

18. $\dfrac{5^2}{1^3}$ Different roots cannot be divided.

19. $\dfrac{4x^5}{2x^2}$ Both roots are x. $4 \div 2 = 2$ $^{5-2=3}$ $= 2x^3$

20. $(3^5)^2$ $^{5 \times 2 = 10}$ $= 3^{10} = 59,049$

21. $(7^2)^0$ $^{2 \times 0 = 0}$ $= 7^0 = 1$ Any number raised to the ^{0} power $= 1$.

22. $(2^2)^2$ $^{2 \times 2 = 4}$ $= 2^4 = 16$

23. $(x^4)^2$ $^{4 \times 2 = 8}$ $= x^8$

24. 5^{-4} $5 = \dfrac{5}{1}$ the reciprocal $= \dfrac{1}{5},$ $5^{-4} = \dfrac{1}{5^4}$

25. 2^{-6} $2 = \dfrac{2}{1}$ the reciprocal $= \dfrac{1}{2},$ $2^{-6} = \dfrac{1}{2^6}$

26. $\left(\dfrac{1}{a}\right)^{-3}$ $\dfrac{1}{a}$ the reciprocal $= \dfrac{a}{1},$ $\left(\dfrac{1}{a}\right)^{-3} = a^3$

114

Answer Keys (cont.)

Chapter 5: Exponents and Exponential Expressions
Practice: Exponent Power (pages 71–72)

1. 5^7

2. 10^{14}

3. a^{20}

4. 25 x 25 x 25 x 25 x 25

5. $b \cdot b \cdot b \cdot b \cdot b \cdot b \cdot b \cdot b \cdot b \cdot b \cdot b \cdot b \cdot b \cdot b \cdot b \cdot b \cdot b \cdot b \cdot b \cdot b$

6. $3(c \cdot c \cdot c \cdot c \cdot c)$

7. $5(d \cdot d \cdot d)y$

8. 9,765,625

9. 10,000,000,000

10. 2,097,152

11. 1,838,265,625

12. It is a shorthand way of writing very large or very small numbers.

13. $35x^7$

14. a^{13}

15. $6x^7$

16. $18b^{10}$

17. 8^2

18. 5^3

19. $2b^2$

20. $4c^3$

21. 1

22. 1

23. $3^{15} = 14,348,907$

24. x^{12}

25. $4^8 = 65,536$

26. $5(3)^3 = 5(27) = 135$

27. $3(6 - 2)^3 = 3(4)^3 = 3(64) = 192$

28. $4x^3 + 6x^3 = 10x^3$

29. $6^{-3} + 7^0 = \dfrac{1}{6^3} + 1 = 1\frac{1}{216}$

30. $7n^4 - 2n^4 = 5n^4$

Answer Keys (cont.)

Chapter 6: Square Roots
Practice: Square Roots (pages 80–81)

1. $\sqrt{4}$ 2   Perfect Square

2. $\sqrt{9}$ 3   Perfect Square

3. $\sqrt{1}$ 1   Perfect Square

4. $\sqrt{25}$ 5   Perfect Square

5. $\sqrt{36}$ 6   Perfect Square

6. $\sqrt{3}$ 1.732050808

7. $\sqrt{2}$ 1.414213562

8. $\sqrt{(25)(9)}$ $(\sqrt{25})(\sqrt{9}) = (5)(3) = 15$

9. $\sqrt{(4)(16)}$ $(\sqrt{4})(\sqrt{16}) = (2)(4) = 8$

10. $\sqrt{16y^2}$ $(y > 0)$ $(\sqrt{16})(\sqrt{y^2}) = (4)(y) = 4y$

11. $(\sqrt{y})(\sqrt{y})$ $y > 0$ $\sqrt{(y)(y)} = \sqrt{y^2} = y$

12. $(\sqrt{3})(\sqrt{12})$ $\sqrt{(3)(12)} = \sqrt{36} = 6$

13. $\sqrt{32}$ $\sqrt{(2)(16)} = (\sqrt{2})(\sqrt{16}) = \sqrt{2}(4) \approx (1.414213562)(4) \approx 5.656854249$

14. $\sqrt{125}$ $(\sqrt{5})(\sqrt{25}) = \sqrt{5}(5) = 2.236067978(5) = 11.18033989$

15. $\sqrt{\dfrac{25}{36}} =$ $\dfrac{\sqrt{25}}{\sqrt{36}} = \dfrac{5}{6}$ 16. $\sqrt{\dfrac{64}{16}} =$ $\dfrac{\sqrt{64}}{\sqrt{16}} = \dfrac{8}{4} = 2$

17. $\sqrt{\dfrac{4}{3}} =$ $\dfrac{\sqrt{4}}{\sqrt{3}} = \left(\dfrac{2}{\sqrt{3}}\right)\left(\dfrac{\sqrt{3}}{\sqrt{3}}\right) = \dfrac{2\sqrt{3}}{\sqrt{3(3)}} = \dfrac{2\sqrt{3}}{\sqrt{9}} = \dfrac{2\sqrt{3}}{3}$

18. $3\sqrt{36} + \sqrt{1} =$ Different numbers under the radical sign; cannot be added.

19. $4\sqrt[5]{x} + 5\sqrt[5]{x}$ $4 + 5 = 9$ so $4\sqrt[5]{x} + 5\sqrt[5]{x} = 9\sqrt[5]{x}$

20. $6\sqrt[5]{x} + \sqrt[2]{x}$ Different indexes cannot be added.

21. $8\sqrt{5} - 4\sqrt{5} =$ $8 - 4 = 4$ so $8\sqrt{5} - 4\sqrt{5} = 4\sqrt{5}$

22. $9\sqrt{2y} - 3\sqrt{2y} =$ $9 - 3 = 6$ so $9\sqrt{2y} - 3\sqrt{2y} = 6\sqrt{2y}$

Chapter 6: Square Roots
Practice: Rooting out the Answers (page 82)

1. C   2. D   3. B   4. A   5. G   6. H   7. E   8. I

9. J   10. F

11. $\sqrt{(16)(9)} = \sqrt{144} = 12$

Answer Keys (cont.)

12. $(\sqrt{3})(\sqrt{48}) = \sqrt{(3)(48)} = \sqrt{144} = 12$

13. $\sqrt{\dfrac{16}{4}} = \dfrac{\sqrt{16}}{\sqrt{4}} = \dfrac{4}{2} = 2$

14. $\dfrac{3}{\sqrt{3}} = \dfrac{3}{\sqrt{3}}\left(\dfrac{\sqrt{3}}{\sqrt{3}}\right) = \dfrac{3\sqrt{3}}{\sqrt{9}} = \dfrac{3\sqrt{3}}{3} = \sqrt{3} \approx 1.732050808$

15. $4\sqrt{144} + 7\sqrt{144} = 11\sqrt{144} = 11(12) = 132$

Chapter 7: Using Algebra to Generalize Patterns
Practice: Moving From Words to Symbols (pages 90–91)

1. A)   13, 21, 34

   B)   To find the next entry, add together the previous two entries. This list of numbers is known as the Fibonnacci sequence and is used often.

2. A)   15, 21, 28

   B)   What would the tenth number in the list be? 55

   C)   To find the entry, add the next higher counting number—from 1st to 2nd added 2, from 2nd to 3rd added 3, etc.

3. A)   If the input is 21, what will the output be?   16

   B)   Describe the rule in words: Subtract 5 from each input to get the output.

   C)   Describe the rule in symbols: If n is the input, then $n - 5$ is the ouput.

4. A)   If the input is -5, what will the output be?   20

   B)   Describe the rule in words: Take the input, square it, and then add the input to get the output.

   C)   Describe the rule in symbols: If n is the input, then $n^2 + n$ is the output.

5. $7x^2$ EXP

6. $2x + 5$ EXP

7. $n + (n + 1) = 15$ EQ

8. $N - 12$ EXP

9. $x - y = \frac{1}{2}(x + y)$ EQ

10. $x = -7$

11. $m = 7$

12. $1 = x$

Answer Keys (cont.)

13. $x = -12$
14. $b = \frac{6}{5}$ or $1\frac{1}{5}$
15. $x = -22$

Chapter 7: Using Algebra to Generalize Patterns
Practice: More Moving From Words to Symbols (pages 92–93)

1. A) 29, 47, 76

   B) To find the next entry, add together the previous two entries.

2. A) 64, 128

   B) What would the tenth number in the list be? 512

   C) To find the next entry, multiply the prior entry times two.

3. A) If the input is 30, what will the output be?   37

   B) Describe the rule in words: Add 7 to each input to get the output.

   C) Describe the rule in symbols: If n is the input, then $n + 7$ is the ouput.

4. A) If the input is 5, what will the output be?   -2

   B) Describe the rule in words: Subtract 7 from the input to get the output.

   C) Describe the rule in symbols: If n is the input, then $n - 7$ is the output.

5. $5x^3$ EXP

6. $4n + 5$ EXP

7. $n + (n - 1) = 15$ EQ

8. $n + 12$ EXP

9. $a - b = \frac{1}{4}(a + b)$ EQ

10. $x = -7$

11. $a = 32$

12. $11 = x$

13. $x = -9$

14. $b = \frac{16}{7} = 2\frac{2}{7}$

15. $x = -10$

Answer Keys (cont.)

Chapter 8: Problem-Solving Strategies
Practice: Problem Solving (pages 100–101)

1. Dan has $10 more than Chris. Together they have $80. How much money does each one have?

$x + (x + 10) = 80$ $2x = 70$ Chris = $35

$x + x + 10 = 80$ $\dfrac{2x}{2} = \dfrac{70}{2}$ Dan = $35 + $10 = $45

$2x + 10 = 80$

$2x + 10 - 10 = 80 - 10$ $x = 35$

2. The concession stand sold twice as much cola as it did orange soda and sold three times as much bottled water as orange soda. A total of 600 drinks were sold. How many bottles of water were sold?

$x + 2x + 3x = 600$

$6x = 600$

$x = 100$

Bottled water is $3x$ so $3(100) = 300$ bottles of water were sold.

3. Most bacteria divide every 20 minutes. Starting with one bacteria, how many bacteria will be present in three hours?

# of Minutes	0	20	40	60	80	100	120	140	160	180
				1 hr.			2 hrs.			3 hrs.
# of Bacteria	1	2	4	8	16	32	64	128	256	512

4. $x + 4 = 0$

$x + 4 - 4 = 0 - 4$

$x = -4$

5. $5b + 3 = 28$

$5b + 3 - 3 = 28 - 3$

$5b = 25$

$\dfrac{5b}{5} = \dfrac{25}{5}$

$b = 5$

Answer Keys (cont.)

6. $2x - 12 = 8$

   $2x - 12 + 12 = 8 + 12$

   $2x = 20$

   $\dfrac{2x}{2} = \dfrac{20}{2}$

   $x = 10$

7. $5y - 1 = 124$

   $5y - 1 + 1 = 124 + 1$

   $5y = 125$

   $\dfrac{5y}{5} = \dfrac{125}{5}$

   $y = 25$

8. A board is 12 feet long. It is sawed into two pieces. One piece is 0.5 feet longer than the other. How many feet long is each piece?

   $x + (x + 0.5) = 12$ ft.

9. Tyrone has four times as many books as Lei. Together they have 50 books. How many books does each student have?

   $L + 4L = 50$

10. There are 12 people on a jury. Four more jurors voted to convict than not to convict the person on trial. How many voted to convict?

    $n + (n + 4) = 12$

11. Laticia had 8 fewer pencils than Kim. They had a total of 20 pencils. How many did each have?

    $k + (k - 8) = 20$

Answer Keys (cont.)

Chapter 8: Problem-Solving Strategies
Practice: What Is the Problem? (pages 102–104)

1A. 7: 76, 8: 84, 9: 92

  B. Teacher check graph. It should represent the equation $y = 8x + 20$

  C. 116 cm

  D. $y = 8x + 20$

2A. $700

  B. $(2 \times 7)(\$50) = \$700$

3A. $y = 8x + 30$, $150 = 8(15) + 30$, 150 cm above the floor

  B. Teacher check graph. It should represent the equation $y = 8x + 30$.

References

References

Brown, R., Dolciani, M., Sorgenfrey, R., Cole, W., (1997). *Algebra structure and method book 1.* Evanston, IL: McDougal Littell.

Chicago Mathematics Project (found online July 2004). *Connected mathematics.* University of Chicago. Found online at: http://www.math.msu.edu/cmp/curriculum/Algebra.htm

Edwards, E. (1990). *Algebra for everyone.* Reston, VA: National Council of Teachers of Mathematics.

Long, L. (1998). *Painless algebra.* Hauppauge, NY: Barron's Educational Series.

National Council of Teachers of Mathematics (NCTM). (2000). *Principles and standards for school mathematics.* Reston, VA: National Council of Teachers of Mathematics.

National Council of Teachers of Mathematics (NCTM). (2004). *Standards and expectations for algebra.* Reston, VA: National Council of Teachers of Mathematics. Found online at: http://www.nctm.org

Freudenthal Institute at the University of Utrecht / University of Wisconsin / NSF (found online July 2004) *Math in context.* http://www.showmecenter.missouri.edu/showme/mic.shtml Encyclopedia Britannica.

Web Resources

Algebra.help. (2001–2004)
http://www.algebrahelp.com/index.jsp

Algebra Solutions
http://www.gomath.com/algebra.html

Awesome Library—Algebra
http://www.awesomelibrary.org/Classroom/Mathematics/Middle-High_School_Math/Algebra.html

Borenson, H. (2001–2004) *Hands on Equations.* Allentown, PA: Borenson and Associates. Found online at: http://www.borenson.com/?src=overture

Brennon, J. (2002) *Understanding algebra.* Found online at: http://www.jamesbrennan.org/algebra/

References (cont.)

Cool Math Sites
http://www.cte.jhu.edu/techacademy/web/2000/heal/mathsites.htm

Ed Helper.com
http://www.edhelper.com/algebra.htm

History of Algebra
http://www.ucs.louisiana.edu/~sxw8045/history.htm

Holt, Rinehart, and Winston Mathematics in Context
http://www.hrw.com/math/mathincontext/index.htm

Interactive Mathematic Miscellany and Puzzles
http://www.cut-the-knot.org/algebra.shtml

Introduction to Algebra
http://www.mathleague.com/help/algebra/algebra.htm

Math Archives: Topics in Mathematics, Algebra
http://www.archives.math.utk.edu/topics/algebra.html

Moses, B. *The algebra project.* Cambridge, MA: The Algebra Project, Inc.
http://www.algebra.org/index.html

Oracle Education Foundation Think Quest Library (2004) Algebra
Found online at: http://library.thinkquest.org/10030/algecon.htm

Reichman, H. and Kohn, M. (2004) *Math made easy.*
Found online at: http://mathmadeeasy.com/algebra.html

Reliable problem solving in all subjects that use mathematics for problem solving. Algebra, Physics, Chemistry... from grade school to grad school and beyond.
http://www2.hawaii.edu/suremath/intro_algebra.html

Show Me Center
http://www.showmecenter.missouri.edu/showme/

SOS Mathematics
http://www.sosmath.com/

Surfing the Net With Kids
http://www.surfnetkids.com/algebra.htm

References (cont.)

The Math Forum Drexel University (1994–2004) K–12 Internet Algebra Resources. Philadelphia, PA.
http://mathforum.org/algebra/k12.algebra.html

University of Akron Theoretical and Applied Mathematics
http://www.math.uakron.edu/~dpstory/mpt_home.html

Real Life Applications of Math

Applied Academics: Applications of Mathematics—Careers
http://www.bced.gov.bc.ca/careers/aa/lessons/math.htm

Exactly How is Math Used in Technology
http://www.math.bcit.ca/examples/index.shtml

Mathematics Association of America—Careers
http://www.maa.org/careers/index.html

NASA Space Link
http://www.spacelink.msfc.nasa.gov/.index.html